Poor Richard's

Almanack

& OTHER WRITINGS

Poor Richard's

Almanack

& OTHER WRITINGS

BENJAMIN FRANKLIN

Edited and with an Introduction by
BOB BLAISDELL

DOVER PUBLICATIONS, INC.
Mineola, New York

Bibliographical Note

Poor Richard's Almanack and Other Writings is a new work, first published by Dover Publications, Inc., in 2013.

Library of Congress Cataloging-in-Publication Data

Franklin, Benjamin, 1706-1790.
   [Poor Richard. Selections]
   Poor Richard's almanack, and other writings / Benjamin Franklin ; edited and with an introduction by Bob Blaisdell.
      p. cm.
   Summary: "A fascinating compilation of weather forecasts, recipes, jokes, and aphorisms, Poor Richard's Almanack debuted in 1732. This new edition presents hundreds of Franklin's maxims, along with selections from the Letters, Autobiography, and Franklin's Way to Wealth. An ideal resource for writers, public speakers, and students, this practical, charming little book will delight all readers with its folk wisdom"—Provided by publisher.
   Includes bibliographical references.
   ISBN-13: 978-0-486-48449-5 (pbk.)
   ISBN-10: 0-486-48449-1
   I. Blaisdell, Robert. II. Title.

PS749.A6 2013
818'.102—dc23

                                                      2013002922

Manufactured in the United States by LSC Communications
48449103   2020
www.doverpublications.com

Contents

Contents

BENJAMIN FRANKLIN

Introduction

The most interesting American who ever lived was born in 1706 and died in 1790. The Boston-born son of a tallow-chandler had two years of schooling and a few years of apprenticeship under his older brother's stern watch before he fled New England at age seventeen and found himself almost penniless and yet ever resourceful in Philadelphia. He became a printer, writer, businessman, community activist, militia-man, scientist, diplomat, and philosopher, as well as a family man, philanderer, and social animal. Though extraordinary, our most famous and respected citizen became regarded in Europe as America's "representative man." As much as any American, he helped develop the idea of "American" as a national identity, and through his official and unofficial diplomacy in the 1750s and '60s he tried to bring about colonial compromise with England before becoming the budding Revolution's most eloquent and important spokesman.

Not only was he a hardworking, serious-minded joker, he was a skeptic in religion and a true believer in humankind. He never stopped developing and discovering new talents or extending his moral thinking; by the end of his long, fulfilling life he became a prominent abolitionist. Because he was able to do seemingly everything he set his mind to, Franklin became a model for all inventive, diligent creative geniuses—but convincingly pretended to be a model for the rest of us too.

Through the collected editions of his work, as the biographer Edmund S. Morgan points out, we have the opportunity today of knowing Franklin's character and life better than anybody who knew him: "He spoke to friends and enemies alike as he speaks to us, in writing. And we have more of what he wrote and of what was written to him than anyone at the time could have had."[1] This anthology, however, is not a biographical representation but focuses instead on only a couple of aspects of his character: his humor, wit, and satire, and his everyday practical common-man advice. From his *Autobiography* we have excerpted several of his anecdotes as well as his great passage on self-improvement. (With the exception of the first entry which concerns the almanac itself, they have been arranged in the chronological order of the years he refers to rather than to the year he composed each various part.) We have included some of his joshing and frankly-spoken letters and many of his particularly funny parodies and literary impersonations. (He was adept at and seemed to enjoy writing fake public letters on human foibles

---

1   Edmund S. Morgan. *Benjamin Franklin.* New Haven: Yale University Press. 2002. 314.

and habits from the point of view of, among others, Philadelphia's women.)

Our most prominent source for this collection is his series of almanacs, which through his cleverness became (after the Bible) the second most popular book in American homes in the eighteenth century. Besides being annual guides to the predicted weather, tides, moon, and stars, he, in the character of Richard Saunders (as he writes in 1747's Preface), "constantly interspers'd *moral* Sentences, *prudent* Maxims, and wise Sayings, many of them containing *much good Sense* in *very few* Words, and therefore apt to leave *strong* and *lasting* Impressions on the Memory of young Persons, whereby they may receive Benefit as long as they live, when both Almanack and Almanack-maker have been long thrown by and forgotten. If I now and then insert a Joke or two, that seem to have little in them, my Apology is, that such may have their Use, since perhaps for their Sake light airy Minds peruse the rest, and so are struck by somewhat of more Weight and Moment. The Verses on the Heads of the Months are also generally design'd to have the same Tendency. I need not tell thee that not many of them are of my own Making. If thou hast any Judgment in Poetry, thou wilt easily discern the Workman from the Bungler. I know as well as thee, that I am no *Poet born;* and it is a Trade I never learnt, nor indeed could learn. *If I make Verses, 'tis in Spight—Of*

Nature and my Stars, I write. Why then should I give my Readers *bad Lines* of my own, when *good Ones* of other People's are so plenty? 'Tis methinks a poor Excuse for the bad Entertainment of Guests, that the Food we set before them, tho' coarse and ordinary, is of *one's own Raising, off one's own Plantation,* &c. when there is Plenty of what is ten times better, to be had in the Market. ——On the contrary, I assure ye, my Friends, that I have procur'd the best I could for ye, and *much Good may't do ye.*"

As for the dating of items: the prefaces and sayings of Poor Richard's of a given year really belong to the previous year, as Franklin printed the Almanacs in the fall for the following year. We have arranged all the pieces chronologically and have usually bracketed a key or descriptive title or suggestive phrase or quotation from the work for easier reference to the often untitled or variously known works, including one of his most famous, the preface to the 1758 almanac, in which Franklin quotes an old man repeating and citing ad nauseam dozens of Poor Richard's sayings. This essay has been known since then as "The Way to Wealth" or "Father Abraham's Speech." We have provided selections from his sayings (maxims, proverbs) from every year (1733–1758) of his *Poor Richard's Almanack;* the selections made simply on the basis of their wit and representativeness of his practical philosophy. As he would remark, he did not always follow his own precepts but found that striving to do so was better than not. As for his prefaces, after several hilarious ones, the busy man seemed to weary of the composing of them, and only occasionally after the 1730s found his jokiness and interest on hand. All the ones included here are complete. We have attempted to retain and reproduce for the most part his attractive and fitful spelling, capitalization, italicization, and punctuation.

—*Bob Blaisdell*

From his *Autobiography*, "My Almanack" (1732)

In 1732 I first published my Almanack, under the Name of *Richard Saunders*; it was continu'd by me about 25 Years, commonly call'd *Poor Richard's Almanack*. I endeavor'd to make it both entertaining and useful, and it accordingly came to be in such Demand that I reap'd considerable Profit from it, vending annually near ten Thousand. And observing that it was generally read, scarce any Neighborhood in the Province being without it, I consider'd it as a proper Vehicle for conveying Instruction among the common People, who bought scarce any other Books. I therefore filled all the little Spaces that occurr'd between the Remarkable Days in the Calendar, with Proverbial Sentences, chiefly such as inculcated Industry and Frugality, as the Means of procuring Wealth and thereby securing Virtue, it being more difficult for a Man in Want to act always honestly, as (to use here one of those Proverbs) *it is hard for an empty Sack to stand upright*. These Proverbs, which contained the Wisdom of many Ages and Nations, I assembled and form'd into a connected Discourse prefix'd to the Almanack of 1757, as the Harangue of a wise old Man to the People attending an Auction. The bringing all these scatter'd Counsels thus into a Focus, enabled them to make greater Impression. The Piece being universally approved was copied in all the Newspapers of the

Continent, reprinted in Britain on a Broadside to be stuck up in Houses, two Translations were made of it in French, and great Numbers bought by the Clergy & Gentry to distribute gratis among their poor Parishioners and Tenants. In Pennsylvania, as it discouraged useless Expense in foreign Superfluities, some thought, it had its share of Influence in producing that growing Plenty of Money which was observable for several Years after its Publication.

—The Autobiography, Part 3

✌

From his *Autobiography,* "a reasonable creature" (1723)

*[Franklin left his hometown Boston in 1723;
he had become a vegetarian in 1722.]*

I believe I have omitted mentioning that, in my first voyage from Boston, being becalmed off Block Island, our people set about catching cod, and hauled up a great many. Hitherto I had stuck to my resolution of not eating animal food, and on this occasion I considered, with my master Tryon, the taking every fish as a kind of unprovoked murder, since none of them had, or ever could do us any injury that might justify the slaughter. All this seemed very reasonable. But I had formerly been a great lover of fish, and, when this came hot out of the frying-pan, it smelt admirably well. I balanced some time between principle and inclination, till I recollected that, when the fish were opened, I saw smaller fish taken out of their stomachs. Then thought I, "If you eat one another, I don't see why we mayn't eat you." So I dined upon cod very heartily, and continued to eat with other people, returning only now and then occasionally to a vegetable diet. So convenient a thing it is to be a *reasonable creature*, since it enables one to find or make a reason for everything one has a mind to do.

—From *Autobiography*, Part 1

༒

From his *Autobiography*, "strong beer" (c. 1725)

[Franklin sailed to London in 1724 and worked in two printing shops there before returning to Philadelphia in 1726.]

At my first admission into this printing-house I took to working at press, imagining I felt a want of the bodily exercise I had been us'd to in America, where presswork is mix'd with composing. I drank only water; the other workmen, near fifty in number, were great guzzlers of beer. On occasion, I carried up and down stairs a large form of types in each hand, when others carried but one in both hands. They wondered to see, from this and several instances, that the Water-American, as they called me, was *stronger* than themselves, who drank *strong* beer! We had an alehouse boy who attended always in the house to supply the workmen. My companion at the press drank every day a pint before breakfast, a pint at breakfast with his bread and cheese, a pint between breakfast and dinner, a pint at dinner, a pint in the afternoon about six o'clock, and another when he had done his day's work. I thought it a detestable custom; but it was necessary, he suppos'd, to drink *strong* beer, that he might be *strong* to labor. I endeavored to convince him that the bodily strength afforded by beer could only be in proportion to the grain or flour of the barley dissolved in the water of which it was made; that there was more flour in a pennyworth of bread; and therefore, if he would eat that with a pint of water, it would give him more strength than a quart of beer.—He drank on, however, and had four or five shillings to pay out of his wages every Saturday night for that muddling liquor; an expense I was free from.— And thus these poor devils keep themselves always under.

—From *Autobiography*, Part 1

A Query, "How shall we judge of the goodness of a writing?" (c. 1728)

How shall we judge of the goodness of a writing? or what qualities should a writing on any subject have, to be good and perfect in its kind?

Answer. To be good it ought to have a tendency to benefit the reader, by improving his virtue or his knowledge. The method should be just; that is, it should proceed regularly from things known to things unknown, distinctly, clearly, and without confusion. The words used should be the most expressive that the language affords, provided they are the most generally understood. Nothing should be expressed in two words that can as well be expressed in one; that is, no synonyms should be used, but the whole be as short as possible, consistent with clearness. The words should be so placed as to be agreeable to the ear in reading: summarily, it should be *smooth, clear* and *short;* for the contrary qualities are displeasing.

—From "Proposals and Queries for the Consideration of the Junto"

Printer's Errors, "this Omission of the letter (n) in that Word, gave us as much Entertainment as any Part of your Paper" (March 13, 1730)

To the Publisher of *The Pennsylvania Gazette*

Printerum est errare.

Sir,

   As your last Paper was reading in some Company where I was present, these Words were taken Notice of in the Article concerning Governor Belcher, *"After which his Excellency, with the Gentlemen trading to New-England, died elegantly at Pontack's."* The Word *died* should doubtless have been *dined*, Pontack's being a noted Tavern and Eating-house in London for Gentlemen of Condition; but this Omission of the letter (n) in that Word, gave us as much Entertainment as any Part of your Paper. One took the Opportunity of telling us, that in a certain Edition of the Bible, the Printer had, where David says I am fearfully and wonderfully made, omitted the Letter (e) in the last Word, so that it was, *I am fearfully and wonderfully mad;* which occasion'd an ignorant Preacher, who took that Text, to harangue his Audience for half an hour on the Subject of Spiritual Madness. Another related to us, that when the Company of Stationers in England had the Printing of the Bible in their Hands, the

Word (not) was left out in the Seventh Commandment, and the whole Edition was printed off with *Thou shalt commit Adultery,* instead of *Thou shalt not, &c.* This material Erratum induc'd the Crown to take the Patent from them which is now held by the King's Printer. The Spectator's Remark upon this Story is, that he doubts many of our modern Gentlemen have this faulty Edition by 'em, and are not made sensible of the Mistake. A Third Person in the Company acquainted us with an unlucky Fault that went through a whole Impression of Common-Prayer-Books; in the Funeral Service, where these Words are, *We shall all be changed in a moment, in the twinkling of an Eye, &c.* the Printer had omitted the (c) in changed, and it read thus, *We shall all be hanged, &c.* And lastly, a Mistake of your Brother News-Printer was mentioned, in *The Speech of James Prouse* written the Night before he was to have been executed, instead of *I die a Protestant,* he has put it, *I died a Protestant.* Upon the whole you came off with the more favourable Censure, because your Paper is most commonly very correct, and yet you were never known to triumph upon it, by publickly ridiculing and exposing the continual Blunders of your Contemporary. Which Observation was concluded by a good old Gentleman in Company, with this general just Remark, That whoever accustoms himself to pass over in Silence the Faults of his Neighbours, shall meet with much better Quarter from the World when he happens to fall into a Mistake himself; for the Satyrical and Censorious, whose Hand is against every Man, shall upon such Occasions have every Man's Hand against him.

I am, *Sir*, your Friend, &c.

J. T.

—*The Pennsylvania Gazette*

৵

From his *Autobiography*, "He that would thrive, Must ask his Wife"
[Franklin was married by common law to Deborah Read Rogers in 1730; she died in 1774.]

We have an English Proverb that says,

> He that would thrive
> Must ask his Wife;

it was lucky for me that I had one as much dispos'd to Industry & Frugality as myself. She assisted me cheerfully in my Business, folding & stitching Pamphlets, tending Shop, purchasing old Linen Rags for the Paper-makers, &c., &c. We kept no idle Servants, our Table was plain & simple, our Furniture of the cheapest. For instance my Breakfast was a long time Bread & Milk, (no Tea) and I ate it out of a twopenny earthen Porringer with a Pewter Spoon. But mark how Luxury will enter Families, and make a Progress, in Spite of Principle. Being call'd one Morning to Breakfast, I found it in a China Bowl with a Spoon of Silver. They had been bought for me without my Knowledge by my Wife, and had cost her the enormous Sum of three and twenty Shillings, for which she had no other Excuse or Apology to make, but that she thought her Husband deserved a Silver Spoon & China Bowl as well as any of his Neighbors. This was the first Appearance of Plate & China in our House, which afterwards in a Course of Years as our Wealth increas'd augmented gradually to several Hundred Pounds in Value.

—The Autobiography, Part 2

ॐ

An Apology for Printers, "all who are angry with me on the Account of printing things they don't like" (June 10, 1731)

Being frequently censur'd and condemn'd by different Persons for printing Things which they say ought not to be printed, I have sometimes thought it might be necessary to make a standing Apology for my self, and publish it once a Year, to be read upon all Occasions of that Nature. Much Business has hitherto hindered the execution of this Design; but having very lately given extraordinary Offence by printing an Advertisement with a certain N.B. at the End of it, I find an Apology more particularly requisite at this Juncture, tho' it happens when I have not yet Leisure to write such a thing in the proper Form, and can only in a loose manner throw those Considerations together which should have been the Substance of it.

I request all who are angry with me on the Account of printing things they don't like, calmly to consider these following Particulars:

1. That the Opinions of Men are almost as various as their Faces; an Observation general enough to become a common Proverb, *So many Men so many Minds.*

2. That the Business of Printing has chiefly to do with Mens Opinions; most things that are printed tending to promote some, or oppose others.

3. That hence arises the peculiar Unhappiness of that Business, which other Callings are no way liable to; they who follow Printing being scarce able to do any thing in their way of getting a Living, which shall not probably give Offence to some, and perhaps to many; whereas the Smith, the Shoemaker, the Carpenter, or the Man of any other Trade, may work indifferently for People of all Persuasions, without offending any of them: and the Merchant may buy and sell with Jews, Turks, Hereticks, and Infidels of all sorts, and get Money by every one of them, without giving

Offence to the most orthodox, of any sort; or suffering the least Censure or Ill-will on the Account from any Man whatever.

4. That it is as unreasonable in any one Man or Set of Men to expect to be pleas'd with every thing that is printed, as to think that nobody ought to be pleas'd but themselves.

5. Printers are educated in the Belief, that when Men differ in Opinion, both Sides ought equally to have the Advantage of being heard by the Publick; and that when Truth and Error have fair Play, the former is always an overmatch for the latter: Hence they chearfully serve all contending Writers that pay them well, without regarding on which side they are of the Question in Dispute.

6. Being thus continually employ'd in serving all Parties, Printers naturally acquire a vast Unconcernedness as to the right or wrong Opinions contain'd in what they print; regarding it only as the Matter of their daily labour: They print things full of Spleen and Animosity, with the utmost Calmness and Indifference, and without the least Ill-will to the Persons reflected on; who nevertheless unjustly think the Printer as much their Enemy as the Author, and join both together in their Resentment.

7. That it is unreasonable to imagine Printers approve of every thing they print, and to censure them on any particular thing accordingly; since in the way of their Business they print such great variety of things

opposite and contradictory. It is likewise as unreasonable what some assert, That Printers ought not to print any Thing but what they approve; since if all of that Business should make such a Resolution, and abide by it, an End would thereby be put to Free Writing, and the World would afterwards have nothing to read but what happen'd to be the Opinions of Printers.

8. That if all Printers were determin'd not to print any thing till they were sure it would offend no body, there would be very little printed.

9. That if they sometimes print vicious or silly things not worth reading, it may not be because they approve such things themselves, but because the People are so viciously and corruptly educated that good things are not encouraged. I have known a very numerous Impression of *Robin Hood's Songs* go off in this Province at 2s. per Book, in less than a Twelvemonth; when a small Quantity of *David's Psalms* (an excellent Version) have lain upon my Hands above twice the Time.

10. That notwithstanding what might be urg'd in behalf of a Man's being allow'd to do in the Way of his Business whatever he is paid for, yet Printers do continually discourage the Printing of great Numbers of bad things, and stifle them in the Birth. I my self have constantly refused to print any thing that might countenance Vice, or promote Immorality; tho' by complying in such Cases with the corrupt Taste of the Majority,

BENJAMIN FRANKLIN

I might have got much Money. I have also always refus'd to print such things as might do real Injury to any Person, how much soever I have been solicited, and tempted with Offers of great Pay; and how much soever I have by refusing got the Ill-will of those who would have employ'd me. I have heretofore fallen under the Resentment of large Bodies of Men, for refusing absolutely to print any of their Party or Personal Reflections. In this Manner I have made my self many Enemies, and the constant Fatigue of denying is almost insupportable. But the Publick being unacquainted with all this, whenever the poor Printer happens either through Ignorance or much Persuasion, to do any thing that is generally thought worthy of Blame, he meets with no more Friendship or Favour on the above Account, than if there were no Merit in't at all. Thus, as Waller says,

> Poets loose half the Praise they would have got
> Were it but known what they discreetly blot;

Yet are censur'd for every bad Line found in their Works with the utmost Severity.

I take leave to conclude with an old Fable, which some of my Readers have heard before, and some have not.

A certain well-meaning Man and his Son, were travelling towards a

Market Town, with an Ass which they had to sell. The Road was bad; and the old Man therefore rid, but the Son went a-foot. The first Passenger they met, asked the Father if he was not ashamed to ride by himself, and suffer the poor Lad to wade along thro' the Mire; this induced him to take up his Son behind him: He had not travelled far, when he met others, who said, they were two unmerciful Lubbers to get both on the Back of that poor Ass, in such a deep Road. Upon this the old Man gets off, and let his Son ride alone. The next they met called the Lad a graceless, rascally young Jackanapes, to ride in that Manner thro' the Dirt, while his aged Father trudged along on Foot; and they said the old Man was a Fool, for suffering it. He then bid his Son come down, and walk with him, and they travell'd on leading the Ass by the Halter; 'till they met another Company, who called them a Couple of sensless Blockheads, for going both on Foot in such a dirty Way, when they had an empty Ass with them, which they might ride upon. The old Man could bear no longer; My Son, said he, it grieves me much that we cannot please all these People; Let us throw the Ass over the next Bridge, and be no farther troubled with him.

Had the old Man been seen acting this last Resolution, he would probably have been call'd a Fool for troubling himself about the different Opinions of all that were pleas'd to find Fault with him: Therefore, tho'

I have a Temper almost as complying as his, I intend not to imitate him in this last Particular. I consider the Variety of Humours among Men, and despair of pleasing every Body; yet I shall not therefore leave off Printing. I shall continue my Business. I shall not burn my Press and melt my Letters.

—*The Pennsylvania Gazette*

꒰

Alice Addertongue, "If to scandalize be really a Crime" (September 12, 1732)

Mr. Gazetteer,

I was highly pleased with your last Week's Paper upon SCANDAL, as the uncommon Doctrine therein preach'd is agreeable both to my Principles and Practice, and as it was published very seasonably to reprove the Impertinence of a Writer in the foregoing Thursday's *Mercury*, who at the Conclusion of one of his silly Paragraphs, laments, forsooth, that the Fair Sex are so peculiarly guilty of this enormous Crime: Every Blockhead ancient and modern, that could handle a Pen, has I think taken upon him to cant in the same senseless Strain. If to scandalize be really a Crime, what do these Puppies mean? They describe it, they dress it up in the most odious frightful and detestable Colours, they represent it as the worst of Crimes, and then roundly and charitably charge the whole Race of Womankind with it. Are they not then guilty of what they condemn, at the same time that they condemn it? If they accuse us of any other Crime, they must necessarily scandalize while they do it: But to scandalize us with being guilty of Scandal, is in itself an egregious Absurdity, and can proceed from nothing but the most consummate Impudence in Conjunction with the most profound Stupidity.

This, supposing, as they do, that to scandalize is a Crime; which you have convinc'd all reasonable People, is an Opinion absolutely erroneous. Let us leave then these Ideot Mock-Moralists, while I entertain you with some Account of my Life and Manners.

I am a young Girl of about thirty-five, and live at present with my Mother. I have no Care upon my Head of getting a Living, and therefore find it my Duty as well as Inclination, to exercise my Talent at CENSURE, for the Good of my Country folks. There was, I am told, a certain generous Emperor, who if a Day had passed over his Head, in which he had conferred no Benefit on any Man, used to say to his Friends, in Latin, *Diem perdidi,* that is, it seems, I have lost a Day. I believe I should make use of the same Expression, if it were possible for a Day to pass in which I had not, or miss'd, an Opportunity to scandalize somebody: But, Thanks be praised, no such Misfortune has befel me these dozen Years.

Yet, whatever Good I may do, I cannot pretend that I first entred into the Practice of this Virtue from a Principle of Publick Spirit; for I remember that when a Child, I had a violent Inclination to be ever talking in my own Praise, and being continually told that it was ill Manners, and once severely whipt for it, the confin'd Stream form'd itself a new Channel, and I began to speak for the future in the Dispraise of others. This I found more agreable to Company, and almost as much so to my self: For what great Difference can there be, between putting your self up, or putting your Neighbour down? Scandal, like other Virtues, is in part its own Reward, as it gives us the Satisfaction of making our selves appear better than others, or others no better than ourselves.

My Mother, good Woman, and I, have heretofore differ'd upon this Account. She argu'd that Scandal spoilt all good Conversation, and I insisted that without it there could be no such Thing. Our Disputes once rose so high, that we parted Tea-Table, and I concluded to entertain my Acquaintance in the Kitchin. The first Day of this Separation we both drank Tea at the same Time, but she with her Visitors in the Parlor. She would not hear of the least Objection to any one's Character, but began a new sort of Discourse in some such queer philosophical Manner as this; I am mightily pleas'd sometimes, says she, when I observe and consider that the World is not so bad as People out of humour imagine it to be.

There is something amiable, some good Quality or other in every body. If we were only to speak of People that are least respected, there is such a one is very dutiful to her Father, and methinks has a fine Set of Teeth; such a one is very respectful to her Husband; such a one is very kind to her poor Neighbours, and besides has a very handsome Shape; such a one is always ready to serve a Friend, and in my Opinion there is not a Woman in Town that has a more agreeable Air and Gait. This fine kind of Talk, which lasted near half an Hour, she concluded by saying, I do not doubt but every one of you have made the like Observations, and I should be glad to have the Conversation continu'd upon this Subject. Just at that Juncture I peep'd in at the Door, and never in my Life before saw such a Set of simple vacant Countenances; they looked somehow neither glad, nor sorry, nor angry, nor pleas'd, nor indifferent, nor attentive; but, (excuse the Simile) like so many blue wooden Images of Rie Doe. I in the Kitchin had already begun a ridiculous Story of Mr. —'s Intrigue with his Maid, and his Wife's Behaviour upon the Discovery; at some Passages we laugh'd heartily, and one of the gravest of Mama's Company, without making any Answer to her Discourse, got up to go and see what the Girls were so merry about: She was follow'd by a Second, and shortly after by a Third, till at last the old Gentlewoman found herself quite alone, and being convinc'd that her Project was impracticable, came her self and finish'd her Tea with us; ever since which Saul also has been among the Prophets, and our Disputes lie dormant.

By Industry and Application, I have made my self the Center of all the Scandal in the Province, there is little stirring but I hear of it. I began the World with this Maxim, That no Trade can subsist without Returns; and accordingly, whenever I receiv'd a good Story, I endeavour'd to give two or a better in the Room of it. My Punctuality in this Way of Dealing gave such Encouragement, that it has procur'd me an incredible deal of Business, which without Diligence and good Method it would be impossible for me to go through. For besides the Stock of Defamation thus naturally flowing in upon me, I practice an Art by which I can pump Scandal out of People that are the least enclin'd that way. Shall I discover my Secret? Yes; to let it die with me would be inhuman.—If I have never heard Ill of some Person, I always impute it to defective Intelligence; for there are none without their Faults, no not one. If she is a Woman, I take the first Opportunity to let all her Acquaintance know I have heard that one of the handsomest or best Men in Town has said something in Praise either of her Beauty, her Wit, her Virtue, or her good Management. If you know any thing of Humane Nature, you perceive that this naturally introduces a Conversation turning upon all her Failings, past, present, and to come. To the same purpose, and with the same Success, I cause every Man of Reputation to be praised before his Competitors in Love, Business, or Esteem on Account of any particular Qualification. Near the Times of Election, if I find it necessary, I commend every Candidate before some of the opposite Party, listning attentively to what is said of him in answer: (But Commendations in this latter Case are not always necessary, and should be used judiciously;) of late Years I needed only observe what they said of one another freely; and having for the Help of Memory taken Account of all Information & Accusations received, whoever peruses my Writings after my Death, may happen to think, that during a certain Term, the People of Pennsylvania chose into all their Offices of Honour and Trust, the veriest Knaves, Fools and Rascals in the whole Province. The Time of Election used to be a busy Time with me, but this Year, with Concern I speak it, People are grown so good natur'd, so intent upon mutual Feasting and friendly Entertainment, that I see no Prospect of much Employment from that Quarter.

I mention'd above, that without good Method I could not go thro' my Business: In my Father's Life-time I had some Instruction in Accompts, which I now apply with Advantage to my own Affairs. I keep a regular Set of Books, and can tell at an Hour's Warning how it stands between me and the World. In my Daybook I enter every Article of Defamation as it is transacted; for Scandals receiv'd in, I give Credit; and when I pay them out again, I make the Persons to whom they respectively relate Debtor. In my Journal, I add to each Story by Way of Improvement, such probable Circumstances as I think it will bear, and in my Ledger the whole is regularly posted.

I suppose the Reader already condemns me in his Heart, for this particular of adding Circumstances; but I justify that part of my Practice thus. 'Tis a Principle with me, that none ought to have a greater Share of Reputation than they really deserve; if they have, 'tis an Imposition upon the Publick: I know it is every one's Interest, and therefore believe they endeavour, to conceal all their Vices and Follies; and I hold, that those People are extraordinary foolish or careless who suffer a Fourth of their Failings to come to publick Knowledge: Taking then the common Prudence and Imprudence of Mankind in a Lump, I suppose none suffer above one Fifth to be discovered: Therefore when I hear of any Person's Misdoing, I think I keep within Bounds if in relating it I only make it three times worse than it is; and I reserve to my self the Privilege of charging them with one Fault in four, which, for aught I know, they may be entirely innocent of. You see there are but few so careful of doing Justice as my self; what Reason then have Mankind to complain of Scandal? In a general way, the worst that is said of us is only half what might be said, if all our Faults were seen.

Your constant Reader,
ALICE ADDERTONGUE

—*The Pennsylvania Gazette*

Poor Richard's Preface, 1733, "my Regard for my good Friend and Fellow-Student, Mr. *Titan Leeds*"

Courteous Reader,

I might in this place attempt to gain thy Favour, by declaring that I write Almanacks with no other View than that of the publick Good; but in this I should not be sincere; and Men are now a-days too wise to be deceiv'd by Pretences how specious soever. The plain Truth of the Matter is, I am excessive poor, and my Wife, good Woman, is, I tell her, excessive proud; she cannot bear, she says, to sit spinning in her Shift of Tow, while I do nothing but gaze at the Stars; and has threatned more than once to burn all my Books and Rattling-Traps (as she calls my Instruments) if I do not make some profitable Use of them for the good of my Family. The Printer has offer'd me some considerable share of the Profits, and I have thus begun to comply with my Dame's desire.

Indeed this Motive would have had Force enough to have made me publish an Almanack many Years since, had it not been overpower'd by my Regard for my good Friend and Fellow-Student, Mr. *Titan Leeds*, whose Interest I was extreamly unwilling to hurt: But this Obstacle (I am far from speaking it with Pleasure) is soon to be removed, since inexorable Death, who was never known to respect Merit, has already prepared the mortal Dart, the fatal Sister has already extended her destroying Shears, and that ingenious Man must soon be taken from us. He dies, by my Calculation made at his Request, on *Oct.* 17. 1733. 3 ho. 29 m. *P.M.* at the very instant of the conjunction of the Sun and Mercury: By his own Calculation he will survive till the 26th of the same Month. This small difference between us we have disputed whenever we have met these 9 Years past; but at length he is inclinable to agree with my Judgment; Which of us is most exact, a little Time will now determine. As therefore these Provinces may not longer expect to see any of his Performances after this Year, I think my self free to take up the Task, and request a share of the publick Encouragement; which I am the more apt to hope for on this Account, that the Buyer of my Almanack may consider himself, not only as purchasing an useful Utensil, but as performing an Act of Charity, to his poor

> *Friend and Servant*
> R. SAUNDERS

*[Titan Leeds, in his next American Almanack (1734), was so
bewildered by his rival almanac-maker that he seriously
responded to Franklin's joking, as we see below.]*

Kind Reader,

Perhaps it may be expected that I should say something concerning an
Almanack printed for the Year 1733, Said to be writ by Poor Richard or
Richard Saunders, who for want of other matter was pleased to tell his
Readers, that he had calculated my Nativity, and from thence predicts my
Death to be the 17th of October, 1733, at 22 min. past 3 o'clock in the
Afternoon, and that these Provinces may not expect to see any more of
his *(Titan Leeds)* Performances, and this precise Predicter, who predicts
to a Minute, proposes to succeed me in Writing of Almanacks; but notwithstanding his false Prediction, I have by the Mercy of God lived to
write a diary for the Year 1734, and to publish the Folly and Ignorance
of this presumptuous Author. Nay, he adds another gross Falsehood in
his Almanack, viz.—*That by my own Calculation, I shall survive until the
26th of the said Month* (October), which is as untrue as the former, for I
do not pretend to that Knowledge, altho' he has usurpt the Knowledge
of the Almighty herein, and manifested himself a Fool and a Liar. And by

the mercy of God I have lived to survive this conceited Scriblers Day and Minute whereon he has predicted my Death; and as I have supplied my Country with Almanacks for three seven Years by past, to general Satisfaction, so perhaps I may live to write when his Performances are Dead.

Thus much from your annual Friend,
TITAN LEEDS

October 18, 1733, 3 *ho.* 33 *min. P.M.*

~

Poor Richard's Sayings for 1733

The poor have little, beggars none, the rich too much, *enough* not one.

God works wonders now & then;
Behold! a Lawyer, an honest Man!

Beware of the young Doctor & the old Barber.

Nothing more like a Fool, than a drunken Man.

Great Talkers, little Doers.

Hunger never saw bad bread.

A good Wife lost is God's gift lost.

From his *Autobiography*, "some Inconsistency in our common Mode of Teaching Languages," (c. 1733)

I had begun in 1733 to study Languages. I soon made myself so much a Master of the French as to be able to read the Books with Ease. I then undertook the Italian. An Acquaintance who was also learning it, us'd often to tempt me to play Chess with him. Finding this took up too much of the Time I had to spare for Study, I at length refus'd to play any more, unless on this Condition, that the Victor in every Game, should have a Right to impose a Task, either in Parts of the Grammar to be got by heart, or in Translation, &c. which Tasks the Vanquish'd was to perform upon Honor before our next Meeting. As we play'd pretty equally we thus beat one another into that Language. I afterwards with a little Painstaking acquir'd as much of the Spanish as to read their Books also. I have already mention'd that I had only one Year's Instruction in a Latin School, and that when very young, after which I neglected that Language entirely. But when I had attained an Acquaintance with the French, Italian and Spanish, I was surpris'd to find on looking over a Latin Testament, that I understood so much more of that Language than I had imagined; which encouraged me to apply myself again to the Study of it, & I met with the more Success, as those preceding Languages had greatly smooth'd my

Way. From these Circumstances I have thought that there is some Inconsistency in our common Mode of Teaching Languages. We are told that it is proper to begin first with the Latin, and having acquir'd that it will be more easy to attain those modern Languages which are deriv'd from it; and yet we do not begin with the Greek in order more easily to acquire the Latin. It is true, that if you can clamber & get to the Top of a Stair-Case without using the Steps, you will more easily gain them in descending: but certainly if you begin with the lowest you will with more Ease ascend to the Top. And I would therefore offer it to the Consideration of those who superintend the Educating of our Youth, whether, since many of those who begin with the Latin, quit the same after spending some Years, without having made any great Proficiency, and what they have learned becomes almost useless, so that their time has been lost, it would not have been better to have begun them with the French, proceeding to the Italian &c. for tho' after spending the same time they should quit the Study of Languages, & never arrive at the Latin, they would however have acquir'd another Tongue or two that being in modern Use might be serviceable to them in common Life.

—*The Autobiography,* Part 3

From his *Autobiography*, "Arriving at moral Perfection" (c. 1733)

[In the most noted passage from his Autobiography, *Franklin described what has become the most famous of all systematic resolutions at self-improvement. He began "the bold and arduous Project of arriving at moral Perfection" in 1733, when he was 27.]*

It was about this time I conceived the bold and arduous Project of arriving at moral Perfection. I wish'd to live without committing any Fault at any time; I would conquer all that either Natural Inclination, Custom, or Company might lead me into. As I knew, or thought I knew, what was right and wrong, I did not see why I might not *always* do the one and avoid the other. But I soon found I had undertaken a Task of more Difficulty than I had imagined: While my Care was employ'd in guarding against one Fault, I was often surpriz'd by another. Habit took the advantage of Inattention. Inclination was sometimes too strong for Reason. I concluded, at length, that the mere speculative Conviction that it was our Interest to be compleatly virtuous, was not sufficient to prevent our Slipping; and that the contrary Habits must be broken, and good Ones acquired and established, before we can have any Dependence on a steady, uniform Rectitude of Conduct. For this purpose I therefore contrived the following Method.—

In the various Enumerations of the moral Virtues I had met with in my Reading, I found the Catalogue more or less numerous, as different Writers included more or fewer Ideas under the same name. Temperance, for example, was by some confined to Eating & Drinking, while by others it was extended to mean the moderating every other Pleasure, Appetite, Inclination, or Passion, bodily or mental, even to our Avarice & Ambition. I propos'd to myself, for the sake of Clearness, to use rather more Names, with fewer Ideas annexed to each, than a few Names with more ideas; and I included under Thirteen Names of Virtues all that at that time occurred to me as necessary or desirable, and annex'd to each a short Precept, which fully expressed the Extent I gave to its Meaning.

These names of Virtues, with their Precepts were:

1. TEMPERANCE.

Eat not to Dullness. Drink not to Elevation.

2. SILENCE.

Speak not but what may benefit others or your self. Avoid trifling conversation.

3. ORDER.

Let all your Things have their Places. Let each Part of your Business have its Time.

4. Resolution.

Resolve to perform what you ought. Perform without fail what you resolve.

5. Frugality.

Make no expense but to do good to others or yourself; *i.e.,* waste nothing.

6. Industry.

Lose no Time.—Be always employ'd in something useful.—Cut off all unnecessary Actions.

7. Sincerity.

Use no hurtful Deceit. Think innocently and justly; and, if you speak, speak accordingly.

8. Justice.

Wrong none, by doing Injuries, or omitting the Benefits that are your Duty.

9. Moderation.

Avoid Extreams. Forbear resenting Injuries so much as you think they deserve.

10. Cleanliness.

Tolerate no Uncleanlness in Body, Cloaths or Habitation.

11. Tranquillity.

Be not disturbed at Trifles, or at Accidents common or unavoidable.

12. Chastity.

Rarely use Venery but for Health or Offspring; Never to Dullness, Weakness, or the Injury of your own or another's Peace or Reputation.

13. Humility.

Imitate Jesus and Socrates.

My intention being to acquire the *Habitude* of all these virtues, I judg'd it would be well not to distract my Attention by attempting the whole at once, but to fix it on one of them at a time; and, when I should be Master of that, then to proceed to another, and so on, till I should have gone through the thirteen. And as the previous Acquisition of some might facilitate the Acquisition of certain others, I arranged them with that view, as they stand above. *Temperance* first, as it tends to procure that Coolness & Clearness of Head, which is so necessary where constant Vigilance was to be kept up, and Guard maintained against the unremitting Attraction of ancient Habits, and the force of perpetual temptations. This being acquired & established, *Silence* would be more easy; and my Desire being to gain Knowledge at the same time that I improved in Virtue, and considering that in conversation it was obtained rather by the use of the ears than of the tongue, & therefore wishing to break a Habit I was getting into of Prattling, Punning & Joking, which only made me acceptable to trifling Company, I gave *Silence* the second place. This and the next, *Order,* I expected would allow me more time for attending to my project and my studies. *Resolution,* once become habitual, would keep me firm in my Endeavors to obtain all the subsequent virtues; *Frugality* & *Industry* freeing me from my remaining Debt, & producing Affluence & Independence, would make more easy the Practice of *Sincerity* & *Justice*, &c., &c. Conceiving then, that, agreeably to the Advice of Pythagoras in his Golden Verses, daily Examination would be necessary, I contriv'd the following method for conducting that examination.

I made a little Book, in which I allotted a Page for each of the virtues. I rul'd each page with red Ink, so as to have seven Columns, one for each Day of the Week, marking each column with a letter for the day. I crossed these columns with thirteen red Lines, marking the beginning of each Line with the first Letter of one of the Virtues, on which line & in its proper Column, I might mark, by a little black Spot, every Fault I found upon Examination to have been committed respecting that Virtue upon that Day.

I determined to give a Week's strict Attention to each of the Virtues successively. Thus in the first Week my great Guard was to avoid every the least Offence against Temperance, leaving the other Virtues to their ordinary Chance, only marking every Evening the Faults of the Day. Thus if in the first Week I could keep my first line marked T clear of Spots, I suppos'd the Habit of that Virtue so much strengthen'd and its opposite weaken'd, that I might venture extending my Attention to include the next, and for the following Week keep both Lines clear of Spots. Proceeding thus to the last, I could go thro' a Course compleat in Thirteen Weeks, and four Courses in a Year.—And like him who having a Garden to weed, does not attempt to eradicate all the bad Herbs at once, which would exceed his Reach and his Strength, but works on each one of the Beds at a time, & having accomplish'd the first proceeds to a second, so I should have (I hoped) the encouraging Pleasure of seeing on my Pages the Progress I made in Virtue, by clearing successively my Lines of their Spots, till in the End by a Number of Courses, I should be happy in viewing a clean Book after a thirteen Weeks daily Examination....

…I always carried my little Book with me. My Scheme of ORDER gave me the most Trouble, and I found, that tho' it might be practicable where a Man's Business was such as to leave the Disposition of his Time, that of a Journeyman Printer, for instance, it was not possible to be exactly observ'd by a Master, who must mix with the World, and often receive People of Busines at their own Hours.—*Order*, too with regard to Places for Things, Papers, &c., I found extreamly difficult to acquire. I had not been early accustomed to it, & having an exceeding good Memory, I was not so sensible of the Inconvenience attending Want of Method. This Article therefore cost me so much painful Attention & my Faults in it vex'd me so much, and I made so little Progress in Amendment, & had such frequent Relapses, that I was almost ready to give up the Attempt, and content my self with a faulty Character in that respect. Like the Man who in buying an Ax of a Smith my Neighbour, desired to have the whole of its Surface as bright as the Edge; the Smith consented to grind it bright for him if he would turn the Wheel. He turn'd while the Smith press'd the broad Face of the Ax hard & heavily on the Stone, which made the Turning of it very fatiguing. The Man came every now & then from the Wheel to see how the Work went on; and at length would take his Ax as it was without further Grinding. No, says the Smith, Turn on, turn on; we shall have it bright by and by; as yet 'tis only speckled. Yes, says the Man; but—*I think I like a speckled Ax best.*—And I believe this may have been the Case with many who having for want of some such Means as I employ'd found the Difficulty of obtaining good, & breaking bad Habits, in other Points of Vice & Virtue, have given up the Struggle, & concluded that *a speckled Ax was best.* For something that pretended to be Reason was every now and then suggesting to me, that such extream Nicety as

BENJAMIN FRANKLIN

I exacted of my self might be a kind of Foppery in Morals, which if it were known would make me ridiculous; that a perfect Character might be attended with the Inconvenience of being envied and hated; and that a benevolent Man should allow a few Faults in himself, to keep his Friends in Countenance. In Truth I found myself incorrigible with respect to *Order*, and now I am grown old, and my Memory bad, I feel very sensibly the want of it. But on the whole, tho' I never arrived at the Perfection I had been so ambitious of obtaining, but fell far short of it, yet I was by the Endeavor made a better and a happier Man than I otherwise should have been, if I had not attempted it. As those who aim at perfect Writing by imitating the engraved Copies, tho' they never reach the wish'd for Excellence of those Copies, their Hand is mended by the Endeavor, and is tolerable while it continues fair & legible.…

My List of virtues contain'd at first but twelve; but a Quaker Friend having kindly inform'd me that I was generally thought proud; that my Pride showed itself frequently in Conversation; that I was not content with being in the right when discussing any Point, but was overbearing, & rather insolent, of which he convinced me by mentioning several instances; I determined endeavoring to cure myself, if I could, of this Vice or Folly among the rest, and I added *Humility* to my list, giving an extensive Meaning to the word.—I cannot boast of much Success in acquiring the reality of this

Virtue, but I had a good deal with regard to the *Appearance* of it. I made it a Rule to forbear all direct Contradiction to the Sentiments of others, and all positive Assertion of my own. I even forbid myself, agreeably to the old Laws of our Junto, the Use of every Word or Expression in the language that imported a fix'd Opinion, such as *certainly, undoubtedly, &c.,* and I adopted, instead of them, *I conceive, I apprehend,* or *I imagine* a thing to be so or so; or *it so appears to me at present.* When another asserted something that I thought an Error, I denied myself the Pleasure of contradicting him abruptly, and of showing immediately some Absurdity in his Proposition; and in answering I began by observing that in certain Cases or Circumstances his Opinion would be right, but in the present case there *appear'd* or *seem'd* to me some difference, &c. I soon found the Advantage of this Change in my Manners; the Conversations I engaged in went on more pleasantly. The modest way in which I propos'd my Opinions procured them a readier Reception and less Contradiction; I had less Mortification when I was found to be in the wrong, and I more easily prevailed with others to give up their Mistakes & join with me when I happened to be in the right. And this Mode, which I at first put on with some Violence to natural Inclination, became at length so easy, and so habitual to me, that perhaps for these fifty years past no one has ever heard a dogmatical Expression escape me. And to this Habit (after my Character of Integrity) I think it principally owing that I had early so much Weight with my Fellow-Citizens when I proposed new Institutions, or Alterations in the old, and so much Influence in public Councils when I became a Member; for I was but a bad Speaker, never eloquent, subject to much hesitation in my choice of Words, hardly correct in Language, and yet I generally carried my Points.

In reality, there is, perhaps, no one of our natural Passions so hard to subdue as *Pride*. Disguise it, struggle with it, beat it down, stifle it, mortify it as much as one pleases, it is still alive, and will every now and then peep out and show itself. You will see it, perhaps, often in this History; for, even if I could conceive that I had compleatly overcome it, I should probably be proud of my Humility.

—The Autobiography, Part 2

ॐ

From his *Autobiography*, "This Modesty in a Sect is perhaps a singular Instance in the History of Mankind" (c. 1733)

These Embarassments that the Quakers suffer'd from having establish'd & published it as one of their Principles, that no kind of War was lawful, and which being once published, they could not afterwards, however they might change their minds, easily get rid of, reminds me of what I think a more prudent Conduct in another Sect among us; that of the Dunkers[2]. I was acquainted with one of its Founders, Michael Welfare, soon after it appear'd. He complain'd to me that they were grievously calumniated by the Zealots of other Persuasions, and charg'd with abominable Principles and Practices to which they were utter Strangers. I told him this had always been the case with new Sects; and that to put a Stop to such Abuse, I imagin'd it might be well to publish the Articles of their Belief and the Rules of their Discipline. He said that it had been propos'd among them, but not agreed to, for this Reason; "When we were first drawn together as a Society, says he, it had pleased God to enlighten our Minds so far, as to see that some Doctrines which we once esteemed Truths were Errors, & that others which we had esteemed Errors were real Truths. From time to time he has been pleased to afford us farther Light, and our Principles have been improving, & our Errors diminishing. Now we are not sure that we are arriv'd at the End of this Progression, and at the Perfection of Spiritual or Theological Knowledge; and we fear that if we should once print our Confession of Faith, we should feel ourselves as if bound &

---

2   A member of the Church of the Brethren or any of the several other original German Baptist denominations practicing trine immersion and love feasts and refusing to take oaths or to perform military service.

confin'd by it, and perhaps be unwilling to receive farther Improvement; and our Successors still more so, as conceiving what we their Elders & Founders had done, to be something sacred, never to be departed from." This Modesty in a Sect is perhaps a singular Instance in the History of Mankind, every other Sect supposing itself in Possession of all Truth, and that those who differ are so far in the Wrong: Like a Man travelling in foggy Weather: Those at some Distance before him on the Road he sees wrapped up in the Fog, as well as those behind him, and also the People in the Fields on each side; but near him all appears clear. Tho' in truth he is as much in the Fog as any of them. To avoid this kind of Embarrassment the Quakers have of late Years been gradually declining the public Service in the Assembly & in the Magistracy. Choosing rather to quit their Power than their Principle.

—The Autobiography, Part 3

༉

Poor Richard's Preface, 1734, "I foretold the Death of my dear old Friend … Mr. Titan Leeds"

[After the printer Titan Leeds responded to the previous year's Preface, Franklin could not resist twitting him again.]

Courteous Readers,

Your kind and charitable Assistance last Year, in purchasing so large an Impression of my Almanacks, has made my Circumstances much more easy in the World, and requires my grateful Acknowledgment. My Wife has been enabled to get a Pot of her own, and is no longer oblig'd to borrow one from a Neighbour; nor have we ever since been without something of our own to put in it. She has also got a pair of Shoes, two new Shifts, and a new warm Petticoat; and for my part, I have bought a second-hand Coat, so good, that I am now not asham'd to go to Town or be seen there. These Things have render'd her Temper so much more pacifick than it us'd to be, that I may say, I have slept more, and more quietly within this last Year, than in the three foregoing Years put together. Accept my hearty Thanks therefor, and my sincere Wishes for your Health and Prosperity.

In the Preface to my last Almanack, I foretold the Death of my dear old Friend and Fellow-Student, the learned and ingenious Mr. Titan Leeds, which was to be on the 17th of October, 1733, 3 h. 29 m. P.M. at the very instant of the conjunction of the Sun and Mercury. By his own Calculation he was to survive till the 26th of the same Month, and expire in the Time of the Eclipse, near 11 a clock, A.M. At which of these Times he died, or whether he be really yet dead, I cannot at this present Writing positively assure my Readers; forasmuch as a Disorder in my own Family demanded my Presence, and would not permit me as I had intended, to be with him in his last Moments, to receive his last Embrace, to close his Eyes, and do the Duty of a Friend in performing the last Offices to the Departed. Therefore it is that I cannot positively affirm whether he be dead or not; for the Stars only show to the Skilful, what will happen in the natural and universal Chain of Causes and Effects; but 'tis well known, that the Events which would otherwise certainly happen at certain Times in the Course of Nature, are sometimes set aside or postpon'd for wise and good Reasons, by the immediate particular Dispositions of Providence; which particular Dispositions the Stars can by no Means discover or foreshow. There is however, (and I cannot speak it without Sorrow) there is the strongest Probability that my dear Friend is no more; for there appears in his Name, as I am assured, an Almanack for the Year 1734, in which I am treated in a very gross and unhandsome Manner; in which I am called a false Predicter, an Ignorant, a conceited Scribler, a Fool, and a Lyar. Mr. Leeds was too well bred to use any Man so indecently and so scurrilously, and moreover his Esteem and Affection for me was extraordinary: So that it is to be feared, that Pamphlet may be only a Contrivance of somebody or other, who hopes perhaps to sell two or three Year's Almanacks still, by the sole Force and Virtue of Mr. Leeds's

Name; but certainly, to put Words into the Mouth of a Gentleman and a Man of Letters, against his Friend, which the meanest and most scandalous of the People might be asham'd to utter even in a drunken Quarrel, is an unpardonable Injury to his Memory, and an Imposition upon the Publick.

Mr. Leeds was not only profoundly skilful in the useful Science he profess'd, but he was a Man of exemplary Sobriety, a most sincere Friend, and an exact Performer of his Word. These valuable Qualifications, with many others, so much endear'd him to me, that although it should be so, that, contrary to all Probability, contrary to my Prediction and his own, he might possibly be yet alive, yet my Loss of Honour as a Prognosticator, cannot afford me so much Mortification, as his Life, Health and Safety would give me Joy and Satisfaction. I am,

> *Courteous and kind Reader,*
> *Your poor Friend and Servant,*
> *R. SAUNDERS*

October 30, 1733

Poor Richard's Sayings for 1734

He does not possess Wealth, it possesses him.

Better slip with foot than tongue.

No man e'er was glorious, who was not laborious.

Would you persuade, speak of Interest, not of Reason.

Where there's Marriage without Love, there will be Love without Marriage.

There have been as great Souls unknown to fame as any of the most famous.

A learned blockhead is a greater blockhead than an ignorant one.

As sore places meet most rubs, proud folks meet most affronts.

꒒

Poetry for January 1734, "good L—d, deliver me"

From a cross neighbour, and a sullen wife,
    A pointless needle, and a broken knife;
From suretyship, and from an empty purse,
    A smoaky chimney, and a jolting horse;

From a dull razor, and an aking head;
   From a bad conscience, and a buggy bed,
A blow upon the elbow and the knee;
   From each of these, good L—d, deliver me.

꙳

Poetry for June 1734, "Why till her marriage day she proved so coy"

When Robin now three days had married been,
   And all his friends and neighbours gave him joy,
This question of his wife he asked then,
   Why till her marriage day she proved so coy!

Indeed said he, 'twas well thou didst not yield,
   For doubtless then my purpose was to leave thee:
O, sir, I once before was so beguil'd,
   And was resolved the next should not deceive me.

꙳

Poetry for October 1734, "Altho' thy teacher act not as he preaches"

Altho' thy teacher act not as he preaches,
   Yet ne'ertheless, if good, do what he teaches;
Good counsel, failing men may give, for why,
   He that's aground knows where the shoal doth lie.

My old friend Berryman oft, when alive,
   Taught others thrift, himself could never thrive:
Thus like the whetstone, many men are wont
   To sharpen others while themselves are blunt.

ॐ

Poetry for December 1734, "He that for sake of Drink neglects his Trade"

By Mrs. Bridget Saunders, my Dutchess, in Answer to the
December Verses of last Year.

He that for sake of Drink neglects his Trade,
   And spends each Night in Taverns till 'tis late,

And rises when the Sun is four hours high,
    And ne'er regards his starving Family;
God in his Mercy may do much to save him.
    But, woe to the poor Wife, whose Lot it is to have him.

ﻬ

Poetry: The Benefit of Going to Law

Dedicated to the Countess of K—t and H-r-d-n.

Two beggars travelling along,
    One blind, the other lame,
Pick'd up an oyster on the way,
    To which they both laid claim:
The matter rose so high, that they
    Resolv'd to go to law,
As often richer fools have done,
    Who quarrel for a straw.

A lawyer took it strait in hand,
    Who knew his business was
To mind nor one nor t'other side,

But make the best o' th' cause,
As always in the law's the case:
    So he his judgment gave,
And lawyer-like he thus resolv'd
    What each of them should have;

Blind plaintif, lame defendant, share
    The friendly laws impartial care.
A shell for him, a shell for thee.
    The middle is the *lawyer's fee.*

—*Poor Richard's Almanack* (1734)

❧

Poor Richard's Preface, 1735

Courteous Reader,

This is the third Time of my appearing in print, hitherto very much to my own Satisfaction, and, I have reason to hope, to the Satisfaction of the Publick also; for the Publick is generous, and has been very charitable and good to me. I should be ungrateful then, if I did not take every Opportunity of expressing my Gratitude; for *ingratum si dixeris, omnia dixeris*[3]: I therefore return the Publick my most humble and hearty Thanks.

Whatever may be the Musick of the Spheres, how great soever the Harmony of the Stars, 'tis certain there is no Harmony among the Stargazers; but they are perpetually growling and snarling at one another like strange Curs, or like some Men at their Wives: I had resolved to keep the Peace on my own part, and affront none of them; and I shall persist in that Resolution: But having receiv'd much Abuse from *Titan Leeds* deceas'd, (*Titan Leeds* when living would not have us'd me so!) I say, having receiv'd much Abuse from the Ghost of *Titan Leeds,* who pretends to be still living, and to write Almanacks in spight of me and my Predictions, I cannot help saying, that tho' I take it patiently, I take it very unkindly. And whatever he may pretend, 'tis undoubtedly true that he is really defunct and dead. First because the Stars are seldom disappointed, never but in the Case of wise Men, *Sapiens dominabitur astris*[4], and they foreshow'd his Death at the Time I predicted it. Secondly, 'Twas requisite and necessary he should die punctually at that Time, for the Honour of Astrology, the Art professed both by him and his Father before him. Thirdly, 'Tis

---

3 If ungrateful, everyone says so
4 A wise one rules the stars

plain to every one that reads his two last Almanacks (for 1734 and '35) that they are not written with that *Life* his Performances use to be written with; the Wit is low and flat, the little Hints dull and spiritless, nothing smart in them but *Hudibras's* Verses against Astrology at the Heads of the Months in the last, which no Astrologer but a *dead one* would have inserted, and no Man living would or could write such Stuff as the rest. But lastly, I shall convince him from his own Words, that he is dead, *(ex ore suo condemnatus est[5])* for in his Preface to his Almanack for 1734, he says, *"Saunders adds another GROSS FALSHOOD in his Almanack, viz. that by my own Calculation I shall survive until the 26th of the said Month October 1733, which is as* untrue *as the former."* Now if it be, as *Leeds* says, *untrue* and a *gross Falshood* that he surviv'd till the 26th of October 1733, then it is certainly *true* that he died *before* that Time: And if he died before that Time, he is dead now, to all Intents and Purposes, any thing he may say to the contrary notwithstanding. And at what Time before the 26th is it so likely he should die, as at the Time by me predicted, *viz.* the 17th of October aforesaid? But if some People will walk and be troublesome after Death, it may perhaps be born with a little, because it cannot well be avoided unless one would be at the Pains and Expence of laying them

---

5   Out of his own mouth was he convicted

in the *Red Sea;* however, they should not presume too much upon the Liberty allow'd them; I know Confinement must needs be mighty irksome to the free Spirit of an Astronomer, and I am too compassionate to proceed suddenly to Extremities with it; nevertheless, tho' I resolve with Reluctance, I shall not long defer, if it does not speedily learn to treat its living Friends with better Manners. I am,

Courteous Reader,
Your obliged Friend and Servant,
R. *SAUNDERS*

October 30, 1734

༃

Poor Richard's Sayings for 1735

A lie stands on one leg, truth on two.

To be humble to Superiors is Duty, to Equals Courtesy, to Inferiors Nobleness.

Pain wastes the Body, Pleasures the Understanding.

A man is never so ridiculous by those Qualities that are his own as by those that he affects to have.

Necessity never made a good bargain.

> Bad Commentators spoil the best of books,
> So God sends meat (they say) the devil Cooks.

Are you angry that others disappoint you? Remember, you cannot depend upon yourself.

⤶

A Man of Sense [Dialogue between Socrates and Crito] (February 11, 1735)

Mr. Franklin,

Being the other Day near the Meeting-House Corner with some Gentlemen, in the open Street, I heard the following Piece of Conversation; and penn'd it down as soon as I came home. I am confident it varies scarce any thing from what really passed; and as it pleased the By-standers, it may possibly please the Publick, if you give it a Place in your Paper.

It not being proper to name the Persons discoursing, I shall call one of them *Socrates*, his manner of Arguing being in my Opinion, somewhat like that of *Socrates*: And, if you please, the other may be *Crito*.

> *I am Yours, &c.*
> *A. A.*

Socrates: Who is that well-dress'd Man that passed by just now?

Crito: He is a Gentleman of this City, esteem'd a *Man of Sense,* but not very honest.

Socrates: The Appellation of *a Man of Sense is of late frequently given, and seems to come naturally into the Character of every Man we are about to praise: But I am at some Loss to know whether a Man who is not honest* can deserve it.

Crito: Yes, doubtless; There are many vicious Men who are nevertheless Men of very good Sense.

Socrates: You are of Opinion, perhaps, that a Man of Knowledge is a *Man of Sense.*

Crito: I am really of that Opinion.

Socrates: Is the Knowledge of Push-pin, or of the Game at Ninepins, or of Cards and Dice, or even of Musick and Dancing, sufficient to constitute the Character of a Man of Sense?

Crito: No certainly; there are many silly People that understand these Things tolerably well.

Socrates: Will the Knowledge of Languages, or of Logic and Rhetoric serve to make a Man of Sense?

Crito: I think not; for I have known very senseless Fellows to be Masters of two or three Languages; and mighty full of their Logic, or their Rhetoric.

Socrates: Perhaps some Men may understand all the Forms and Terms of Logic, or all the Figures of Rhetoric, and yet be no more able to convince or to perswade, than others who have not learnt those Things?

Crito: Indeed I believe they may.

Socrates: Will not the Knowledge of the Mathematicks, Astronomy, and Natural Philosophy, those sublime Sciences, give a Right to the Character of a *Man of Sense?*

Crito: At first Sight I should have thought they might: But upon Recollection I must own I have known some Men, Masters of those Sciences, who, in the Management of their Affairs, and *Conduct of their Lives,* have acted very weakly, I do not mean viciously but foolishly; and therefore I cannot find in my Heart to allow 'em the Character of *Men of Sense.*

Socrates: It seems then, that no Knowledge will serve to give this Character, but the Knowledge of our *true Interest;* that is, of what is best to be done in all the Circumstances of Humane Life, in order to arrive at our main End in View, HAPPINESS.

Crito: I am of the same Opinion. And now, as to the Point in Hand, I suppose you will no longer doubt whether a vicious Man may deserve the Character of a Man of Sense, since 'tis certain that there are many Men who *know* their true Interest, &c., and are therefore *Men of Sense,* but are nevertheless vicious and dishonest Men, as appears from the whole

Tenour of their Conduct in Life.

Socrates: Can Vice consist with any Man's true Interest, or contribute to his Happiness?

Crito: No certainly; for in Proportion as a Man is vicious he loses the Favour of God and Man, and brings upon himself many Inconveniences, the least of which is capable of marring and demolishing his Happiness.

Socrates: How then does it appear that those vicious Men have the Knowledge we have been speaking of, which constitutes a *Man of Sense,* since they act directly contrary?

Crito: It appears by their Discoursing perfectly well upon the Subjects of Vice and Virtue, when they occur in Conversation, and by the just Manner in which they express their Thoughts of the pernicious Consequences of the one, and the happy Effects of the other.

Socrates: Is it the Knowledge of all the Terms and Expressions proper to be used in Discoursing well upon the Subject of making a good Shoe, that constitutes a Shoemaker; or is it the Knowing how to go about it and do it?

Crito: I own it is the latter, and not the former.

Socrates: And if one who could only *talk finely* about Shoe-making, were to be set to work, would he not presently discover his Ignorance in that Art?

Crito: He would, I confess.

Socrates: Can the Man who is only able to talk justly of Virtue and Vice, and to say that "Drunkenness, Gluttony and Lewdness destroy a Man's Constitution; waste his Time and Substance, and bring him under many Misfortunes, (to the Destruction of his Happiness) which the contrary Virtues would enable him to avoid"; but notwithstanding his talking thus, continues in those Vices; can such a Man deserve the Character of a Temperate and Chaste Man? Or does not that Man rather deserve it, who having a *thorough Sense* that what the other has said is true, *knows* also *how* to resist the Temptation to those Vices, and embrace Virtue with a hearty and steady Affection?

Crito: The latter, I acknowledge. And since Virtue is really the true Interest of all Men; and some of those who talk well of it, do not put it in Practice, I am now inclined to believe they speak only by rote, retailing to us what they have pick'd out of the Books or Conversation of wise and virtuous Men; but what having never enter'd or made any Impression on their Hearts, has therefore no Influence on the Conduct of their Lives.

Socrates: Vicious Men, then, do not appear to have that Knowledge which constitutes the *Man of Sense*.

Crito: No, I am convinced they do not deserve the Name. However, I am afraid, that instead of *defining* a Man of Sense we have now entirely *annihilated* him: For if the Knowlege of his true Interest in all Parts of the Conduct of Life, and a constant Course of Practice agreeable to it, are essential to his Character, I do not know where we shall find him.

Socrates: There seems no necessity that to be a Man of Sense, he should never make a Slip in the Path of Virtue, or in Point of Morality; provided he is sensible of his Failing and diligently applys himself to rectify what is done amiss, and to prevent the like for the future. The best Arithmetician may err in casting up a long Account; but having found that Error, he *knows how* to mend it, and immediately does so; and is notwithstanding that Error, an Arithmetician; But he who always blunders, and cannot correct his Faults in Accounting, is no Arithmetician; nor is the habitually-vicious Man a *Man of Sense*.

Crito: But methinks 'twill look hard, that all other Arts and Sciences put together, and possess'd by one Man in the greatest Perfection, are not able to dignify him with the Title of a *Man of Sense*, unless he be also a Man of Virtue.

Socrates: We shall agree, perhaps, that one who is a *Man of Sense,* will not spend his Time in learning such Sciences as, if not useless in themselves, will probably be useless to him?

Crito: I grant it.

Socrates: And of those which may be useful to him, that is, may contribute to his Happiness, he ought, if he is a Man of Sense, to know how to make them so.

Crito: To be sure.

Socrates: And of those which may be useful, he will not (if he is a Man of Sense) acquire all, except that One only which is the most useful of all, to wit, the Science of Virtue.

Crito: It would, I own, be inconsistent with his Character to do so.

Socrates: It seems to follow then, that the vicious Man, tho' Master of many Sciences, must needs be an ignorant and foolish Man; for being, as he is vicious, of consequence unhappy, either he has acquired only the useless Sciences, or having acquired such as might be useful, he knows not how to make them contribute to his Happiness; and tho' he may have every other Science, he is ignorant that the SCIENCE OF VIRTUE is of more worth, and of more consequence to his Happiness than all the rest put together. And since he is ignorant of what *principally* concerns him, tho' it has been told him a thousand Times from Parents, Press, and Pulpit, the Vicious Man however learned, cannot be a *Man of Sense,* but is a Fool, a Dunce, and a Blockhead.

—*The Pennsylvania Gazette*

Reply to a Piece of Advice, "A Man does not act contrary to his Interest by Marrying" (March 4, 1735)

Mr. Franklin,

In your Paper of the 18th past, some Verses were inserted, said to be design'd as a PIECE OF ADVICE to a good Friend. As this *Piece of Advice,* if it had been intended for a particular Friend alone, might have been as well convey'd to him privately; I suppose the Author by getting it publish'd, thinks it may be of Use to great Numbers of others, in his Friend's Circumstances. The import of it is, "That 'tis mighty silly for a single Man to change his State; for as soon as his Wishes are crown'd, his expected Bliss dissolves into Cares in Bondage, which is a compleat Curse; That only Fools in Life wed, for every Woman is a Tyrant: That he who marries, acts contrary to his Interest, loses his Liberty and his Friends, and will soon perceive himself undone; and that the best of the Sex are no better than a Plague." So ill-natur'd a Thing must have been written, either by some forlorn old Batchelor, or some cast-away Widower, that has got the Knack of drowning all his softer Inclinations in his Bowl or his Bottle. I am grown old and have made abundance of Observations, and I have had three Wives my self; so that from both Experience and Observation I can say, that this Advice is wrong and untrue in every

Particular. It is wrong to assert that *'tis silly in a single Man to change his State:* For what old Batchelor can die without Regret and Remorse, when he reflects upon his Death-bed, that the inestimable Blessing of Life and Being has been communicated by Father to Son through all Generations from *Adam* down to him, but in him it stops and is extinguished; and that the *Humane Race divine* would be no more, for any Thing he has done to continue it; he having, like the wicked Servant, *wrapt up and hid his Talent in a Napkin,* (i.e. his Shirt Tail,) while his Neighbours the Good and Faithful Servants, had some of them produced Five and some Ten. I say such an one shall not only die with Regret, but he may justly fear a severe Punishment. Nor is it true that *as soon as a Man weds, his expected Bliss dissolves into slavish Cares and Bondage.* Every Man that is really a Man is Master of his own Family; and it cannot be Bondage to have another submit to one's Government. If there be any Bondage in the Case, 'tis the Woman enters into it, and not the Man. And as to the Cares, they are chiefly what attend the bringing up of Children; and I would ask any Man who has experienced it, if they are not the most delightful Cares in the World; and if from that Particular alone, he does not find the Bliss of a double State much greater, instead of being less than he expected. In short this *Bondage* and these *Cares* are like the Bondage of having a beautiful and fertile Garden, which a Man takes great Delight in; and the Cares are the Pleasure he finds in cultivating it, and raising as many beautiful and useful Plants from it as he can. And if common Planting and Gardening be an Honourable Employment, (as 'tis generally allow'd, since the greatest Heroes have practic'd it without any Diminution to their Glory) I think *Human Planting* must be more Honourable, as the Plants to be raised are more excellent in their Nature, and to bring them to Perfection requires the greater Skill and Wisdom.

As to the Adviser's next Insinuation, that *only Fools wed, and every Woman is a Tyrant;* 'tis a very severe and undutiful Reflection upon his own Father and Mother; and since he is most likely to know best the Affairs of his own Family, I shall not contradict him in that particular, so far as relates to his own Relations: for perhaps his Aversion to a Wife arises from observing how his Mamma treated his Daddy; for she might be a *Xantippe* tho' he was no *Socrates*; it being probable that a wise Man would have instill'd sounder Principles into his Son. But in general I utterly dissent from him, and declare, that I scarce ever knew a Man who knew how to command in a proper Manner, but his Wife knew as well how to show a becoming Obedience. And there are in the World infinitely more He-Tyrants than She-Ones.

In the next Place he insinuates, that *a Man by marrying, acts contrary to his Interest, loses his Liberty and his Friends, and soon finds himself undone.*

In which he is as much mistaken as in any of the rest. A Man does not act contrary to his Interest by Marrying; for I and Thousands more know very well that we could never thrive till we were married; and have done well ever since; What we get, the Women save; a Man being fixt in Life minds his Business better and more steadily; and he that cannot thrive married, could never have throve better single; for the Idleness and Negligence of Men is more frequently fatal to Families, than the Extravagance of Women. Nor does a Man *lose his Liberty* but encrease it; for when he has no Wife to take Care of his Affairs at Home, if he carries on any Business there, he cannot go Abroad without a Detriment to that; but having a Wife, that he can confide in, he may with much more Freedom be abroad, and for a longer Time; thus the Business goes on comfortably, and the good Couple relieve one another by turns, like a faithful Pair of Doves. Nor does he *lose Friends* but gain them, by prudently marrying; for there are all the Woman's Relations added to his own, ready to assist and encourage the new-married Couple; and a Man that has a Wife and Children, is sooner trusted in Business, and can have Credit longer and for larger Sums than if he was single, inasmuch as he is look'd upon to be more firmly settled, and under greater Obligations to behave honestly, for his Family's Sake.

I have almost done with our Adviser, for he says but one thing more; to wit, *that the best of the Sex are no better than Plagues.* Very hard again upon his poor Mother, who tho' she might be the best Woman in the World, was, it seems, in her graceless Son's Opinion, no better than a Pestilence. Certainly this Versifyer never knew what a Woman is! He must be, as I conjectur'd at first, some forlorn old Batchelor. And if I could conjure, I believe I should discover, that his Case is like that of many other old He-Maids I have heard of. Such senseless Advice as this can have no Effect upon them; 'tis nothing like this, that deters them from marrying. But having in some of their first Attempts upon the kinder Sort of the Fair Sex, come off with Shame and Disgrace, they persuade themselves that they are, (and perhaps they are) really Impotent: And so durst not marry, for fear of those dishonourable Decorations of the Head, which they think it the inevitable Fate of a Fumbler to wear. Then, like the Fox who could not use his Tail, (but the Fox had really lost it) they set up for *Advisers*, as the Gentleman I have been dealing with; and would fain persuade others, that the Use of their own Tails is more mischievous than beneficial. But I shall leave him to Repentance …

I am, Sir,

> Your most humble Servant,
> *A. A.*

> —*The Pennsylvania Gazette*

Poor Richard's Preface, 1736

Loving Readers,

Your kind Acceptance of my former Labours, has encouraged me to continue writing, tho' the general Approbation you have been so good as to favour me with, has excited the Envy of some, and drawn upon me the Malice of others. These Ill-willers of mine, despited at the great Reputation I gain'd by exactly predicting another Man's Death, have endeavour'd to deprive me of it all at once in the most effectual Manner, by reporting that I my self was never alive. They say in short, *That there is no such a Man as I am;* and have spread this Notion so thoroughly in the Country, that I have been frequently told it to my Face by those that don't know me. This is not civil Treatment, to endeavour to deprive me of my very Being, and reduce me to a Non-entity in the Opinion of the publick. But so long as I know my self to walk about, eat, drink and sleep, I am satisfied that *there is really such a Man as I am,* whatever they may say to the contrary: And the World may be satisfied likewise; for if there were no such Man as I am, how is it possible I should appear publickly to hundreds of People, as I have done for several Years past, in print? I need not, indeed, have taken any Notice of so idle a Report, if it had not been for the sake of my Printer, to whom my Enemies are pleased to ascribe my

Productions; and who it seems is as unwilling to father my Offspring, as I am to lose the Credit of it: Therefore to clear him entirely, as well as to vindicate my own Honour, I make this publick and serious Declaration, which I desire may be believed, to wit, *That what I have written heretofore, and do now write, neither was nor is written by any other Man or Men, Person or Persons whatsoever.* Those who are not satisfied with this, must needs be very unreasonable.

My Performance for this Year follows; it submits itself, kind Reader, to thy Censure, but hopes for thy Candor, to forgive its Faults. It devotes itself entirely to thy Service, and will serve thee faithfully: And if it has the good Fortune to please its Master, 'tis Gratification enough for the Labour of

Poor
R. SAUNDERS

꙳

Poor Richard's Sayings for 1736

None preaches better than the ant, and she says nothing.

Do not do that which you would not have known.

Never praise your Cyder, Horse, or Bedfellow.

Wealth is not his that has it, but his that enjoys it.

Fish & Visitors stink in 3 days.

The absent are never without fault, nor the present without excuse.

Creditors have better memories than debtors.

Lovers, Travellers, and Poets, will give money to be heard.

He that speaks much, is much mistaken.

'Tis easy to see, hard to foresee.

స

Poor Richard's Preface, 1737

Courteous and kind Reader,

This is the fifth Time I have appear'd in Publick, chalking out the future Year for my honest Countrymen, and foretelling what shall, and what may, and what may not come to pass; in which I have the Pleasure to find that I have given general Satisfaction. Indeed, among the Multitude of our astrological Predictions, 'tis no wonder if some few fail; for, without any Defect in the Art itself, 'tis well known that a small Error, a single wrong Figure overseen in a Calculation, may occasion great Mistakes: But however we Almanack-makers may *miss it* in other Things, I believe it will be generally allow'd *That we always hit the Day of the Month,* and that I suppose is esteem'd one of the most useful Things in an Almanack.

As to the Weather, if I were to fall into the Method my Brother *J—n* sometimes uses, and tell you, *Snow here or in New England,—Rain here or in South-Carolina,—Cold to the Northward,—Warm to the Southward,* and the like, whatever Errors I might commit, I should be something more secure of not being detected in them: But I consider, it will be of no Service to any body to know what Weather it is 1000 miles off, and therefore I always set down positively what Weather my Reader will have, be he where he will at the time. We modestly desire only the favourable Allowance of *a day or two before* and *a day or two after* the precise Day against which the Weather is set; and if it does not come to pass accordingly, let the Fault be laid upon the Printer, who, 'tis very like, may have transpos'd or misplac'd it, perhaps for the Conveniency of putting in his Holidays: And since, in spight of all I can say, People will give him great part of the Credit of making my Almanacks, 'tis but reasonable he should take some share of the Blame.

I must not omit here to thank the Publick for the gracious and kind Encouragement they have hitherto given me: But if the generous Purchaser of my Labours could see how often his *Fi'-pence* helps to light up the comfortable Fire, line the Pot, fill the Cup and make glad the Heart of a poor Man and an honest good old Woman, he would not think his Money ill laid out, tho' the Almanack of his

Friend and Servant, R. SAUNDERS

were one half blank Paper.

༚

Poor Richard's Sayings for 1737

Tell a miser he's rich, and a woman she's old, you'll get no money of one, nor kindness of t'other.

The Creditors are a superstitious sect, great observers of set days and times.

The greatest monarch on the proudest throne, is oblig'd to sit upon his own arse.

The noblest question in the world is *What Good may I do in it?*

Nothing is so popular as GOODNESS.

Don't go to the doctor with every distemper, nor to the lawyer with every quarrel, nor to the pot for every thirst.

Well done is better than well said.

At the working man's house hunger looks in but dares not enter.

He that can compose himself, is wiser than he that composes books.

᠅

Poor Richard's Preface, 1738

Preface by Mistress SAUNDERS

Dear Readers,

My good Man set out last Week for *Potowmack*, to visit an old Stargazer of his Acquaintance, and see about a little Place for us to settle and end our Days on. He left the Copy of his Almanack seal'd up, and bid me send it to the Press. I suspected something, and therefore as soon as he was gone, I open'd it, to see if he had not been flinging some of his old Skitts at me. Just as I thought, so it was. And truly, (for want of somewhat else to say, I suppose) he had put into his Preface, that his Wife *Bridget*— was this, and that, and t'other.—What a peasecods! cannot I have a little Fault or two, but all the Country must see it in print! They have already been told, at one time that I am proud, another time that I am loud, and that I have got a new Petticoat, and abundance of such kind of stuff; and now, forsooth! all the World must know, that *Poor Dick's* Wife has lately taken a fancy to drink a little Tea now and then. A mighty matter, truly, to make a Song of! 'Tis true; I had a little Tea of a Present from the Printer last Year; and what, must a body throw it away? In short, I thought the Preface was not worth a printing, and so I fairly scratch'd it all out, and I believe you'll like our Almanack never the worse for it.

Upon looking over the Months, I see he has put in abundance of foul Weather this Year; and therefore I have scatter'd here and there, where I could find room, some *fair, pleasant, sunshiny,* &c. for the Good-Women to dry their Clothes in. If it does not come to pass according to my Desire, I have shown my Good-will, however; and I hope they'll take it in good part.

I had a Design to make some other Corrections; and particularly to change some of the Verses that I don't very well like; but I have just now unluckily broke my Spectacles; which obliges me to give it you as it is, and conclude

Your loving Friend,
BRIDGET SAUNDERS

࿔

Poor Richard's Sayings for 1738

There are three faithful friends, an old wife, an old dog, and ready money.

Eat to please thyself, but dress to please others.

Buy what thou hast no need of; and e'er long thou shalt sell thy necessaries.

As we must account for every idle word, so we must for every idle silence.

If you do what you should not, you must hear what you would not.

You may be more happy than Princes, if you will be more virtuous.

Keep your eyes wide open before marriage, half shut afterwards.

None but the well-bred man knows how to confess a fault, or acknowledge himself in an error.

Sell not virtue to purchase wealth, nor Liberty to purchase power.

If thou hast wit & learning, add to it Wisdom and Modesty.

Great talkers should be cropt, for they've no need of ears.

Since I cannot govern my own tongue, tho' within my own teeth, how can I hope to govern the tongues of others?

Search others for their virtues, thy self for thy vices.

Who has deceiv'd thee so oft as thy self?

Wink at small faults; remember thou hast great ones.

Write with the learned, pronounce with the vulgar.

> If you wou'd not be forgotten
>> As soon as you are dead and rotten,
> Either write things worth reading,
>> Or do things worth the writing.

Reading makes a full Man, Meditation a profound Man, discourse a clear Man.

Poor Richard's Preface, 1739

Kind Reader,

Encouraged by thy former Generosity, I once more present thee with an Almanack, which is the 7th of my Publication.—While thou art putting Pence in my Pocket, and furnishing my Cottage with Necessaries, *Poor Dick* is not unmindful to do something for thy Benefit. The Stars are watch'd as narrowly as old *Bess* watch'd her Daughter, that thou mayst be acquainted with their Motions, and told a Tale of their Influences and Effects, which may do thee more good than a Dream of last Year's Snow.

Ignorant Men wonder how we Astrologers foretell the Weather so exactly, unless we deal with the old black Devil. Alas! 'tis as easy as pissing abed. For Instance; The Stargazer peeps at the Heavens thro' a long Glass: He sees perhaps TAURUS, or the great Bull, in a mighty Chase, stamping on the Floor of his House, swinging his Tail about, stretching out his Neck, and opening wide his Mouth. 'Tis natural from these Appearances to judge that this furious Bull is puffing, blowing, and roaring. Distance being consider'd, and Time allow'd for all this to come down, there you have Wind and Thunder. He spies perhaps VIRGO (or the Virgin;) she turns her Head round as it were to see if any body observ'd her; then crouching down gently, with her Hands on her Knees, she looks wistfully for a while right forward. He judges rightly what she's about: And having calculated the Distance and allow'd Time for its Falling, finds that next Spring we shall have a fine *April* shower. What can be more natural and easy than this? I might instance the like in many other particulars; but this may be sufficient to prevent our being taken for Conjurers. O the wonderful Knowledge to be found in the Stars! Even the smallest Things are written there, if you had but Skill to read. When my Brother *J—m—n* erected a Scheme to know which was best for his sick Horse, to sup a

new-laid Egg, or a little Broth, he found that the Stars plainly gave their Verdict for Broth, and the Horse having sup'd his Broth;—Now, what do you think became of that Horse? You shall know in my next.

Besides the usual Things expected in an Almanack, I hope the profess'd Teachers of Mankind will excuse my scattering here and there some instructive Hints in Matters of Morality and Religion. And be not thou disturbed, O grave and sober Reader, if among the many serious Sentences in my Book, thou findest me trifling now and then, and talking idly. In all the Dishes I have hitherto cook'd for thee, there is solid Meat enough for thy Money. There are Scraps from the Table of Wisdom, that will if well digested, yield strong Nourishment to thy Mind. But squeamish Stomachs cannot eat without Pickles; which, 'tis true are good for nothing else, but they provoke an Appetite. The Vain Youth that reads my Almanack for the sake of an idle Joke, will perhaps meet with a serious Reflection, that he may ever after be the better for.

Some People observing the great Yearly Demand for my Almanack, imagine I must by this Time have become rich, and consequently ought to call myself *Poor Dick* no longer. But, the Case is this, When I first begun to publish, the Printer made a fair Agreement with me for my Copies, by Virtue of which he runs away with the greatest Part of the Profit.—However, much good may't do him; I do not grudge it him; he is a Man I have a great Regard for, and I wish his Profit ten times greater than it is. For I am, dear Reader, his, as well as thy

Affectionate Friend,
R. Saunders

~

Poor Richard's Sayings for 1739

Sin is not hurtful because it is forbidden but it is forbidden because it's hurtful. Nor is a Duty beneficial because it is commanded, but it is commanded, because it's beneficial.

Blessed is he that expects nothing, for he shall never be disappointed.

Hear no ill of a Friend, nor speak any of an Enemy.

Industry need not wish.

No Resolution of Repenting hereafter, can be sincere.

He that falls in love with himself, will have no Rivals.

~

Poor Richard's Preface, 1740

Courteous Reader,

You may remember that in my first Almanack, published for the Year 1733, I predicted the Death of my dear Friend *Titan Leeds,* Philomat, to happen that Year on the 17th Day of *October,* 3 h. 29 m. *P.M.* The good Man, it seems, died accordingly: But *W.B.* and *A.B.* have continued to publish Almanacks in his Name ever since; asserting for some Years that he was still living; At length when the Truth could no longer be conceal'd from the World, they confess his Death in their Almanack for 1739, but pretend that he died not till last Year, and that before his Departure he had furnished them with Calculations for 7 Years to come. Ah, My Friends, these are poor Shifts and thin Disguises; of which indeed I should have taken little or no Notice, if you had not at the same time accus'd me as a false Predictor; an Aspersion that the more affects me, as my whole Livelyhood depends on a contrary Character.

But to put this Matter beyond Dispute, I shall acquaint the World with a Fact, as strange and surprizing as it is true; being as follows, *viz.*

On the 4th Instant, towards midnight, as I sat in my little Study writing this Preface, I fell fast asleep; and continued in that Condition for some time, without dreaming any thing, to my Knowledge. On awaking,

I found lying before me the following Letter, *viz.*

Dear Friend SAUNDERS,

My Respect for you continues even in this separate State, and I am griev'd to see the Aspersions thrown on you by the Malevolence of avaricious Publishers of Almanacks, who envy your Success. They say your Prediction of my Death in 1733 was false, and they pretend that I remained alive many Years after. But I do hereby certify, that I did actually die at that time, precisely at the Hour you mention'd, with a Variation only of *5 min. 53 sec.* which must be allow'd to be no great matter in such Cases. And I do farther declare that I furnish'd them with no Calculations of the Planets Motions, &c. seven Years after my Death, as they are pleased to give out: so that the Stuff they publish as an Almanack in my Name is no more mine than 'tis yours.

You will wonder perhaps, how this Paper comes written on your Table. You must know that no separate Spirits are under any Confinement till after the final Settlement of all Accounts. In the mean time we wander where we please, visit our old Friends, observe their Actions, enter sometimes into their Imaginations, and give them Hints waking or sleeping that may be of Advantage to them. Finding you asleep, I entred your left Nostril, ascended into your Brain, found out where the Ends of those

Nerves were fastned that move your right Hand and Fingers, by the Help of which I am now writing unknown to you; but when you open your Eyes, you will see that the Hand written is mine, tho' wrote with yours.

The People of this Infidel Age, perhaps, will hardly believe this Story. But you may give them these three Signs by which they shall be convinc'd of the Truth of it. About the middle of *June* next, *J. J—n,* Philomat, shall be openly reconciled to the *Church of Rome,* and give all his Goods and Chattles to the Chappel, being perverted by a certain *Country School-master.* On the *7th* of *September* following my old Friend *W. B—t* shall be sober 9 Hours, to the Astonishment of all his Neighbours: And about the same time *W.B.* and *A.B.* will publish another Almanack in my Name, in spight of Truth and Common-Sense.

As I can see much clearer into Futurity, since I got free from the dark Prison of Flesh, in which I was continually molested and almost blinded with Fogs arising from Tiff, and the Smoke of burnt Drams; I shall in kindness to you, frequently give you Informations of things to come, for the Improvement of your Almanack: Being Dear *Dick,*

Your affectionate Friend, T. Leeds

For my own part I am convinc'd that the above Letter is genuine. If the Reader doubts of it, let him carefully observe the three Signs; and if they do not actually come to pass, believe as he pleases.

I am his humble Friend,
R. SAUNDERS

October 7, 1739

ॐ

Poor Richard's Sayings for 1740

Observe all men; thy self most.

> A Flatterer never seems absurd:
> The Flatter'd always take his Word.

When you speak to a man, look on his eyes; when he speaks to thee, look on his mouth.

Fear not Death; for the sooner we die, the longer shall we be immortal.

> In other men we faults can spy,
>   And blame the mote that dims their eye;
> Each little speck and blemish find;
>   To our own stronger errors blind.

To bear other People's Afflictions, every one has Courage enough, and to spare.

> When befriended, remember it:
> When you befriend, forget it.

Lend Money to an Enemy, and thou'lt gain him, to a Friend and thou'lt lose him.

> An open Foe may prove a curse;
> But a pretended friend is worse.

There are lazy Minds as well as lazy Bodies.

> Those who in quarrels interpose,
> Must often wipe a bloody nose.

Promises may get thee Friends, but Nonperformance will turn them into Enemies.

Poor Richard's Sayings for 1741

Learn of the skilful: He that teaches himself, hath a fool for his master.

At 20 years of age the Will reigns; at 30 the Wit; at 40 the Judgment.

If you would keep your Secret from an enemy, tell it not
to a friend.

᠈ᢒ

Poor Richard's Preface, 1742

Courteous Reader,

   This is the ninth Year of my Endeavours to serve thee in the Capac-
ity of a Calendar-Writer. The Encouragement I have met with must be
ascrib'd, in a great Measure, to your Charity, excited by the open honest
Declaration I made of my Poverty at my first Appearance.

   This my Brother *Philomaths* could, without being Conjurers, discover;
and *Poor Richard's* Success, has produced ye a *Poor Will,* and a Poor Robin; and no doubt *Poor John,* &c. will follow, and we shall all be in Name
what some Folks say we are already *in Fact,* A Parcel of *poor Almanack
Makers.* During the Course of these nine Years, what Buffetings have
I not sustained! The Fraternity have been all in Arms. Honest *Titan*,
deceas'd, was rais'd, and made to abuse his old Friend. Both Authors and
Printers were angry. Hard Names, and many, were bestow'd on me. They
deny'd me to be the Author of my own Works; declar'd there never was
any such Person; asserted that I was dead 60 Years ago; prognosticated

my Death to happen within a Twelvemonth: with many other malicious Inconsistences, the Effects of blind Passion, Envy at my Success; and a vain Hope of depriving me (dear Reader) of thy wonted Countenance and Favour.—*Who knows him?* they cry: *Where does he live?*—

But what is that to them? If I delight in a private Life, have they any Right to drag me out of my Retirement? I have good Reasons for concealing the Place of my Abode. 'Tis time for an old Man, as I am, to think of preparing for his great Remove. The perpetual Teasing of both Neighbours and Strangers, to calculate Nativities, give Judgments on Schemes, erect Figures, discover Thieves, detect Horse-Stealers, describe the Route of Run-aways and stray'd Cattle; The Croud of Visitors with a 1000 trifling Questions; *Will my Ship return safe? Will my Mare win the Race? Will her next Colt be a Pacer? When will my Wife die? Who shall be my Husband, and HOW LONG first? When is the best time to cut Hair, trim Cocks, or sow Sallad?* These and the like Impertinences I have now neither Taste nor Leisure for. I have had enough of 'em. All that these angry Folks can say, will never provoke me to tell them where I live. I would eat my Nails first.

My last Adversary is *J. J—n*, Philomat, who *declares and protests* (in his Preface, 1741) that the *false Prophecy put in my Almanack, concerning him, the Year before, is altogether* false and untrue: *and that I am one of Baal's false Prophets.* This *false, false Prophecy* he speaks of, related to his

Reconciliation with the Church of *Rome*; which, notwithstanding his Declaring and Protesting, is, I fear, too true. Two Things in his elegiac Verses confirm me in this Suspicion. He calls the First of *November* by the Name of *All Hallows Day.* Reader; does not this smell of Popery? Does it in the least savour of the pure Language of Friends? But the plainest Thing is; his Adoration of Saints, which he confesses to be his Practice, in these Words, page 4.

> *When any Trouble did me befal,*
> *To my dear Mary then I would call:*

Did he think the whole World were so stupid as not to take Notice of this? So ignorant as not to know, that all Catholicks pay the highest Regard to the *Virgin-Mary?* Ah! Friend John, We must allow you to be a Poet, but you are certainly no Protestant. I could heartily wish your Religion were as good as your Verses.

RICHARD SAUNDERS

༄

Poor Richard's Sayings for 1742

Have you somewhat to do to-morrow; do it to-day.

> If thou dost ill, the joy fades, not the pains;
> If well, the pain doth fade, the joy remains.

Ill Customs & bad Advice are seldom forgotten.

He that riseth late, must trot all day, and shall scarce overtake his business at night.

To err is human, to repent divine, to persist devilish.

One good Husband is worth two good Wives; for the scarcer things are the more they're valued.

> Ben beats his Pate, and fancies wit will come;
> But he may knock, there's no body at home.

Poor Richard's Sayings for 1743

How few there are who have courage enough to own their Faults, or resolution enough to mend them!

> In prosperous fortunes be modest and wise,
>   The greatest may fall, and the lowest may rise:
> But insolent People that fall in disgrace,
>   Are wretched and no-body pities their Case.

How many observe Christ's Birth-day! How few, his Precepts! O! 'tis easier to keep Holidays than Commandments.

Experience keeps a dear school, yet Fools will learn in no other.

Ah simple Man! when a boy two precious jewels were given thee, Time, and good Advice; one thou hast lost, and the other thrown away.

Let all Men know thee, but no man know thee thoroughly: Men freely ford that see the shallows.

> Speak with contempt of none, from slave to king,
> The meanest Bee hath, and will use, a sting.

The World is full of fools and faint hearts; and yet every one has courage enough to bear the misfortunes, and wisdom enough to manage the Affairs of his neighbour.

⌘

Poor Richard's Sayings for 1744

Where there's no Law, there's no Bread.

If you'd lose a troublesome Visitor, lend him Money.

What you would seem to be, be really.

Drive thy Business, or it will drive thee.

God heals, and the Doctor takes the Fees.

Fear God, and your Enemies will fear you.

Industry, Perseverance, & Frugality, make Fortune yield.

Those who are fear'd, are hated.

Who is strong? He that can conquer his bad Habits. Who is rich? He that rejoices in his Portion.

Tart Words make no Friends: a spoonful of honey will catch more flies than a Gallon of Vinegar.

Sloth (like Rust) consumes faster than Labour wears: the used Key is always bright.

Keep thou from the Opportunity, and God will keep thee from the Sin.

๛

Poetry: Epitaph on a Scolding Wife by her Husband

Here my poor Bridgets's Corps doth lie,
She is at rest,—and so am I.

—Poor Richard's Almanack (1744)

Poor Richard's Sayings for 1745

Many complain of their Memory, few of their Judgment.

To God we owe fear and love; to our neighbours justice and charity; to our selves prudence and sobriety.

'Tis easier to prevent bad habits than to break them.

He's a Fool that cannot conceal his Wisdom.

Beware of little Expences, a small Leak will sink a great Ship.

All blood is alike ancient.

You may talk too much on the best of subjects.

No gains without pains.

Every Man has Assurance enough to boast of his honesty, few of their Understanding.

> He who buys need have 100 Eyes,
> but one's enough for him that sells the Stuff.

Great spenders are bad lenders.

It's common for Men to give 6 pretended Reasons instead of one real one.

There are no fools so troublesome as those that have wit.

As often as we do good, we sacrifice.

⌁

Letter to a Young Friend, "you should *prefer old Women* to young ones" (June 25, 1745)

My dear Friend,

I know of no Medicine fit to diminish the violent natural Inclinations you mention; and if I did, I think I should not communicate it to you. Marriage is the *proper* Remedy. It is the most natural State of Man, and therefore the State in which you are most likely to find solid Happiness. Your Reasons against entring into it at present, appear to me not well-founded. The circumstantial Advantages you have in View by postponing it, are not only uncertain, but they are small in comparison with that of the Thing itself, the being married and settled. It is the Man and Woman united that make the compleat human Being. Separate, she wants his Force of Body and Strength of Reason; he, her Softness, Sensibility and acute Discernment. Together they are more likely to succeed in the World. A single Man has not nearly the Value he would have in that State of Union. He is an incomplete Animal. He resembles the odd Half of a Pair of Scissars. If you get a prudent healthy Wife, your Industry in your Profession, with her good Economy, will be a Fortune sufficient.

But if you will not take this Counsel, and persist in thinking a Commerce with the Sex inevitable, then I repeat my former Advice, that in all your Amours you should *prefer old Women to young ones.* You call this a Paradox, and demand my Reasons. They are these:

1st. Because as they have more Knowledge of the World and their Minds are better stor'd with Observations, their Conversation is more improving and more lastingly agreable.

2d. Because when Women cease to be handsome, they study to be good. To maintain their Influence over Men, they supply the Diminution of Beauty by an Augmentation of Utility. They learn to do a 1000 Services small and great, and are the most tender and useful of all Friends when you are sick. Thus they continue amiable. And hence there is hardly such a thing to be found as an old Woman who is not a good Woman.

3d. Because there is no hazard of Children, which irregularly produc'd may be attended with much Inconvenience.

4th. Because thro' more Experience, they are more prudent and discreet in conducting an Intrigue to prevent Suspicion. The Commerce with them is therefore safer with regard to your Reputation. And with regard to theirs, if the Affair should happen to be known, considerate People might be rather inclin'd to excuse an old Woman who would kindly take care of a young Man, form his Manners by her good Counsels, and prevent his ruining his Health and Fortune among mercenary Prostitutes.

5th. Because in every Animal that walks upright, the Deficiency of the Fluids that fill the Muscles appears first in the highest Part: The Face first grows lank and wrinkled; then the Neck; then the Breast and Arms; the lower Parts continuing to the last as plump as ever: So that covering all above with a Basket, and regarding only what is below the Girdle, it is impossible of two Women to know an old from a young one. And as in the dark all Cats are grey, the Pleasure of corporal Enjoyment with an old Woman is at least equal, and frequently superior, every Knack being by Practice capable of Improvement.

6th. Because the Sin is less. The debauching a Virgin may be her Ruin, and make her for Life unhappy.

7th. Because the Compunction is less. The having made a young Girl miserable may give you frequent bitter Reflections; none of which can attend the making an *old* Woman *happy*.

8thly and Lastly They are so grateful!!

Thus much for my Paradox. But still I advise you to marry directly; being sincerely

Your affectionate Friend,

B. F.

—Writings

Poor Richard's Sayings for 1746

The most exquisite Folly is made of Wisdom spun too fine.

Vice knows she's ugly, so puts on her Mask.

It's the easiest Thing in the World for a Man to deceive himself.

Good Sense is a Thing all need, few have, and none think they want.

A Plowman on his Legs is higher than a Gentleman on his Knees.

The Sting of a Reproach, is the Truth of it.

Want of Care does us more Damage than Want of Knowledge.

Poor Richard's Preface, 1747

Courteous Reader,

This is the 15th Time I have entertain'd thee with my annual Productions; I hope to thy Profit as well as mine. For besides the astronomical Calculations, and other Things usually contain'd in Almanacks, which have their daily Use indeed while the Year continues, but then become of no Value, I have constantly interspers'd *moral* Sentences, *prudent* Maxims, and wise Sayings, many of them containing *much good Sense* in *very few* Words, and therefore apt to leave *strong* and *lasting* Impressions on the Memory of young Persons, whereby they may receive Benefit as long as they live, when both Almanack and Almanack-maker have been long thrown by and forgotten. If I now and then insert a Joke or two, that seem to have little in them, my Apology is, that such may have their Use, since perhaps for their Sake light airy Minds peruse the rest, and so are struck by somewhat of more Weight and Moment. The Verses on the Heads of the Months are also generally design'd to have the same Tendency. I need not tell thee that not many of them are of my own Making. If thou hast any Judgment in Poetry, thou wilt easily discern the Workman from the Bungler. I know as well as thee, that I am no *Poet born;* and it is a Trade I never learnt, nor indeed could learn. *If I make Verses, 'tis in Spight—Of Nature and my Stars, I write.* Why then should I give my Readers *bad Lines* of my own, when *good Ones* of other People's are so plenty? 'Tis methinks a poor Excuse for the bad Entertainment of Guests, that the Food we set before them, tho' coarse and ordinary, is of *one's own Raising, off one's own Plantation,* &c. when there is Plenty of what is ten times better, to be had in the Market.—On the contrary, I assure ye, my Friends, that I have procur'd the best I could for ye, and *much Good may't do ye.*

I cannot omit this Opportunity of making honourable Mention of the late deceased Ornament and Head of our Profession, Mr. JACOB TAYLOR, who for upwards of 40 Years (with some few Intermissions only) supply'd the good People of this and the neighbouring Colonies, with the most compleat Ephemeris and most accurate Calculations that have hitherto appear'd in *America.*—He was an ingenious Mathematician, as well as an expert and skilful Astronomer; and moreover, no mean Philosopher, but what is more than all, He was a PIOUS and an HONEST Man. *Requiescat in pace.*

I am thy poor Friend, to serve thee,
R. *SAUNDERS*

Poor Richard's Sayings for 1747

A good Example is the best sermon.

> A quiet Conscience sleeps in Thunder,
> but Rest and Guilt live far asunder.

A Mob's a Monster; Heads enough, but no Brains.

We are not so sensible of the greatest Health as of the least Sickness.

He that won't be counsell'd, can't be help'd.

Write Injuries in Dust, Benefits in Marble.

A Father's a Treasure; a Brother's a Comfort; a Friend is both.

The Speech of Miss Polly Baker, "Can it be a Crime (in the Nature of Things I mean) to add to the Number of the King's Subjects?" (April 1747)

The SPEECH of Miss Polly Baker, before a Court of Judicature, at Connecticut in New England, where she was prosecuted the fifth Time for having a Bastard Child; which influenced the Court to dispense with her Punishment, and induced one of her Judges to marry her the next Day.

May it please the Honourable Bench to indulge me a few Words: I am a poor unhappy Woman; who have no Money to Fee Lawyers to plead for me, being hard put to it to get a tolerable Living. I shall not trouble your Honours with long Speeches; for I have not the presumption to expect, that you may, by any Means, be prevailed on to deviate in your Sentence from the Law, in my Favour. All I humbly hope is, that your Honours would charitably move the Governor's Goodness on my Behalf, that my Fine may be remitted. This is the Fifth Time, Gentlemen, that I have been dragg'd before your Courts on the same Account; twice I have paid heavy Fines, and twice have been brought to public Punishment, for want of Money to pay those Fines. This may have been agreeable to the Laws; I do not dispute it: But since Laws are sometimes unreasonable in themselves, and therefore repealed; and others bear too hard on the Subject in particular Circumstances; and therefore there is left a Power somewhere to dispense with the Execution of them; I take the Liberty to say, that I think this Law, by which I am punished, is both unreasonable in itself, and particularly severe with regard to me, who have always lived an inoffensive Life in the Neighbourhood where I was born, and defy my Enemies (if I have any) to say I ever wrong'd Man, Woman, or Child. Abstracted from the Law, I cannot conceive (may it please your Honours) what the Nature of my Offence is.

I have brought Five fine Children into the World, at the Risque of my Life: I have maintained them well by my own Industry, without burthening the Township, and could have done it better, if it had not been for the heavy Charges and Fines I have paid. Can it be a Crime (in the Nature of Things I mean) to add to the Number of the King's Subjects, in a new Country that really wants People? I own I should think it rather a Praise worthy, than a Punishable Action. I have debauch'd no other Woman's Husband, nor inticed any innocent Youth: These Things I never was charged with; nor has any one the least cause of Complaint against me, unless, perhaps the Minister, or the Justice, because I have had Children without being Married, by which they have miss'd a Wedding Fee. But, can even this be a Fault of mine? I appeal to your Honours. You are pleased to allow I don't want Sense; but I must be stupid to the last Degree, not to prefer the honourable State of Wedlock, to the Condition I have lived in. I always was, and still am, willing to enter into it; I doubt not my Behaving well in it, having all the Industry, Frugality, Fertility, and Skill in Oeconomy, appertaining to a good Wife's Character. I defy any Person to say I ever Refused an Offer of that Sort: On the contrary, I readily Consented to the only Proposal of Marriage that ever was made me, which was when I was a Virgin; but too easily confiding in the Person's Sincerity that made it, I unhappily lost my own Honour, by trusting to his; for he got me with Child, and then forsook me: That very Person you all know; he is now become a Magistrate of this County; and I had hopes he would have appeared this Day on the Bench, and have endeavoured to moderate the Court in my Favour; then I should have scorn'd to have mention'd it; but I must Complain of it as unjust and unequal, that my Betrayer and Undoer, the first Cause of all my Faults and Miscarriages (if they must be deemed such) should be advanced to Honour and Power, in the same Government that punishes my Misfortunes with Stripes and Infamy. I shall be told, 'tis like, that were there no Act of Assembly in the Case, the Precepts of Religion are violated by my Transgressions. If mine, then, is a religious Offence, leave it, Gentlemen, to religious Punishments. You have already excluded me from all the Comforts of your Church Communion: Is not that sufficient? You believe I have offended Heaven, and must suffer eternal Fire: Will not that be sufficient? What need is there, then, of your additional Fines and Whippings? I own, I do not think as you do; for, if I thought, what you call a Sin, was really such, I would not presumptuously commit it. But how can it be believed, that Heaven is angry at my having Children, when, to the little done by me towards it, God has been pleased to add his divine Skill and admirable Workmanship in the Formation of their Bodies, and crown'd it by furnishing them with rational and immortal Souls?

Forgive me, Gentlemen, if I talk a little extravagantly on these Matters; I am no Divine: But if you, great Men (*Turning to some Gentlemen of the Assembly, then in Court*), must be making Laws, do not turn natural and useful Actions into Crimes, by your Prohibitions. Reflect a little on the horrid Consequences of this Law in particular: What Numbers of procur'd Abortions! and how many distress'd Mothers have been driven, by the Terror of Punishment and public Shame, to imbrue, contrary to Nature, their own trembling Hands in the Blood of their helpless Offspring! Nature would have induc'd them to nurse it up with a Parent's Fondness. 'Tis the Law therefore, 'tis the Law itself that is guilty of all these Barbarities and Murders. Repeal it then, Gentlemen; let it be expung'd for ever from your Books.

And on the other hand, take into your wise Consideration, the great and growing Number of Batchelors in the Country, many of whom, from the mean Fear of the Expence of a Family, have never sincerely and honourably Courted a Woman in their Lives; and by their Manner of Living, leave unproduced (which I think is little better than Murder) Hundreds of their Posterity to the Thousandth Generation. Is not theirs a greater Offence against the Public Good, than mine? Compel them then, by a Law, either to Marry, or pay double the Fine of Fornication every Year. What must poor young Women do, whom Custom has forbid to sollicit the Men, and who cannot force themselves upon Husbands, when the Laws take no Care to provide them any, and yet severely punish if they do their Duty without them? Yes, Gentlemen, I venture to call it a Duty; 'tis the Duty of the first and great Command of Nature, and of Nature's God, Increase and multiply: A Duty, from the steady Performance of which nothing has ever been able to deter me; but for its Sake, I have hazarded the Loss of the public Esteem, and frequently incurr'd public Disgrace and Punishment; and therefore ought, in my humble Opinion, instead of a Whipping, to have a Statue erected to my Memory.

—Writings

༄

Poor Richard's Sayings for 1748

> To Friend, Lawyer, Doctor, tell plain your whole Case;
> Nor think on bad Matters to put a good Face:
> How can they advise, if they see but a Part?
> 'Tis very ill driving black Hogs in the dark.

How happy is he, who can satisfy his hunger with any food, quench his thirst with any drink, please his ear with any musick, delight his eye with any painting, any sculpture, any architecture, and divert his mind with any book or any company! How many mortifications must he suffer, that cannot bear any thing but beauty, order, elegance & perfection! Your man of taste, is nothing but a man of distaste.

༄

Advice to a Young Tradesman, Written by an Old One, "Remember that *time* is Money" (c. 1748)

To my Friend A. B.—

As you have desired it of me, I write the following Hints, which have been of Service to me, and may, if observed, be so to you.

Remember that *time* is Money. He that can earn Ten Shillings a Day by his Labour, and goes abroad, or sits idle one half of that Day, tho' he spends but Sixpence during his Diversion or Idleness, ought not to reckon That the only Expence; he has really spent or rather thrown away Five Shillings besides.

Remember that *credit* is Money. If a Man lets his Money lie in my Hands after it is due, he gives me the Interest, or so much as I can make of it during that Time. This amounts to a considerable Sum where a Man has good and large Credit, and makes good Use of it.

Remember that Money is of a prolific generating Nature. Money can beget Money, and its Offspring can beget more, and so on. Five Shillings turn'd, is Six: Turn'd again, 'tis Seven and Three Pence; and so on 'til it becomes an Hundred Pound. The more there is of it, the more it produces every Turning, so that the Profits rise quicker and quicker. He that kills a breeding Sow, destroys all her Offspring to the thousandth Generation. He that murders a Crown, destroys all it might have produc'd, even Scores of Pounds.

Remember that Six Pounds a Year is but a Groat a Day. For this little Sum (which may be daily wasted either in Time or Expence unperceiv'd) a Man of Credit may on his own Security have the constant Possession and Use of an Hundred Pounds. So much in Stock briskly turn'd by an industrious Man, produces great Advantage.

Remember this Saying, That the good Paymaster is Lord of another Man's Purse. He that is known to pay punctually and exactly to the Time he promises, may at any Time, and on any Occasion, raise all the Money his Friends can spare. This is sometimes of great Use: Therefore never keep borrow'd Money an Hour beyond the Time you promis'd, lest a Disappointment shuts up your Friends Purse forever.

The most trifling Actions that affect a Man's Credit, are to be regarded. The Sound of your Hammer at Five in the Morning or Nine at Night, heard by a Creditor, makes him easy Six Months longer. But if he sees you at a Billiard Table, or hears your Voice in a Tavern, when you should be at Work, he sends for his Money the next Day. Finer Cloaths than he or his Wife wears, or greater Expence in any particular than he affords himself, shocks his Pride, and he duns you to humble you. Creditors are a kind of People, that have the sharpest Eyes and Ears, as well as the best Memories of any in the World.

Good-natur'd Creditors (and such one would always chuse to deal with if one could) feel Pain when they are oblig'd to ask for Money. Spare 'em that Pain, and they will love you. When you receive a Sum of Money, divide it among 'em in Proportion to your Debts. Don't be asham'd of paying a small Sum because you owe a greater. Money, more or less, is always welcome; and your Creditor had rather be at the Trouble of receiving Ten Pounds voluntarily brought him, tho' at ten different Times or Payments, than be oblig'd to go ten Times to demand it before he can receive it in a Lump. It shews, besides, that you are mindful of what you owe; it makes you appear a careful as well as an honest Man; and that still encreases your Credit.

Beware of thinking all your own that you possess, and of living accordingly. 'Tis a mistake that many People who have Credit fall into. To prevent this, keep an exact Account for some Time of both your Expences and your Incomes. If you take the Pains at first to mention Particulars, it will have this good Effect; you will discover how wonderfully small trifling Expences mount up to large Sums, and will discern what might have been, and may for the future be saved, without occasioning any great Inconvenience.

In short, the Way to Wealth, if you desire it, is as plain as the Way to Market. It depends chiefly on two Words, *industry* and *frugality*; i.e., Waste neither *Time* nor *Money*, but make the best Use of both. He that gets all he can honestly, and saves all he gets (necessary Expences excepted) will certainly become *rich*; If that Being who governs the World, to whom all should look for a Blessing on their Honest Endeavours, doth not in his wise Providence otherwise determine.

An Old Tradesman

—Writings

Poor Richard's Sayings for 1749

Drink does not drown *Care*, but waters it, and makes it grow faster.

Doing an Injury puts you below your Enemy; *Revenging* one makes you but *even* with him; *Forgiving* it sets you *above* him.

If *Passion* drives, let *Reason* hold the reins.

Words may shew a man's Wit, but *Actions* his Meaning.

Having been poor is no shame, but being ashamed of it is.

All would live long, but none would be old.

శా

Poor Richard's Preface, 1750

The Hope of acquiring lasting FAME, is, with many Authors, a most powerful Motive to Writing. Some, tho' few, have succeeded; and others, tho' perhaps fewer, may succeed hereafter, and be as well known to Posterity by their Works, as the Antients are to us. We *Philomaths*, as ambitious of Fame as any other Writers whatever, after all our painful Watchings and laborious Calculations, have the constant Mortification to see our Works thrown by at the End of the Year, and treated as mere waste Paper. Our only Consolation is, that short-lived as they are, they out-live those of most of our Contemporaries.

Yet, condemned to renew the *Sisyphean* Toil, we every Year heave another heavy Mass up the Muses Hill, which never can the Summit reach, and soon comes tumbling down again.

This, kind Reader, is my seventeenth Labour of the Kind. Thro' thy continued Good-will, they have procur'd me, if no *Bays*, at least *Pence*; and the latter is perhaps the better of the two; since 'tis not improbable that a Man may receive more solid Satisfaction from *Pudding*, while he is *living*, than from *Praise*, after he is *dead*.

In my last, a few Faults escap'd; some belong to the Author, but most to the Printer: Let each take his Share of the Blame, confess, and amend for the future. In the second Page of *August*, I mention'd 120 as the next perfect Number to 28; it was wrong, 120 being no perfect Number; the next to 28 I find to be 496. The first is 6; let the curious Reader, fond of mathematical Questions, find the fourth. In the 2d Page of *March*, in some Copies, the Earth's Circumference was said to be nigh 4000, instead of 24000 Miles, the Figure 2 being omitted at the Beginning. This was Mr. Printer's Fault; who being also somewhat niggardly of his Vowels, as well as profuse of his Consonants, put in one Place, among the Poetry, *mad*, instead of *made*, and in another *wrapp'd*, instead of *warp'd*; to the utter demolishing of all Sense in those Lines, leaving nothing standing but the Rhime. These, and some others, of the like kind, let the Readers forgive, or rebuke him for, as to their Wisdom and Goodness shall seem meet: For in such Cases the Loss and Damage is chiefly to the Reader, who, if he does not take my Sense at first Reading, 'tis odds he never gets it; for ten to one he does not read my Works a second Time.

Printers indeed should be very careful how they omit a Figure or a Letter: For by such Means sometimes a terrible Alteration is made in the Sense. I have heard, that once, in a new Edition of the *Common Prayer,* the following Sentence, *We shall all be changed in a Moment, in the Twinkling of an Eye;* by the Omission of a single Letter, became, *We shall all be hanged in a Moment,* &c. to the no small Surprize of the first Congregation it was read to.

May this Year prove a happy One to Thee and Thine, is the hearty Wish of, Kind Reader,

> *Thy obliged Friend,*
> R. SAUNDERS

Poor Richard's Sayings for 1750

Genius without Education is like Silver in the Mine.

He that spills the Rum, loses that only; He that drinks it, often loses both that and himself.

'Tis a Shame that your Family is an Honour to you! You ought to be an Honour to your Family.

What an admirable Invention is Writing, by which a Man may communicate his Mind without opening his Mouth, and at 1000 Leagues Distance, and even to future Ages, only by the Help of 22 Letters, which may be joined 5852616738497664000 Ways, and will express all Things in a very narrow Compass. 'Tis a Pity this excellent Art has not preserved the Name and Memory of its Inventor.

Glass, China, and Reputation, are easily crack'd, and never well mended.

There are three Things extreamly hard, Steel, a Diamond and to know one's self.

Poor Richard's Sayings for 1751

Youth is pert and positive, *Age* modest and doubting: So Ears of Corn when young and light, stand bolt upright, but hang their Heads when weighty, full, and ripe.

Drunkenness, that worst of Evils, makes some Men Fools, some Beasts, some Devils.

To-day is Yesterday's Pupil.

Friendship increases by visiting Friends, but by visiting seldom.

Not to oversee Workmen, is to leave them your Purse open.

'Tis easier to suppress the first Desire, than to satisfy all that follow it.

❧

Homily, "Money lost may be found"

The *Romans* were 477 Years, without so much as a Sun-dial to show the Time of Day: The first they had was brought from *Sicily*, by *Valerius Messala:* One hundred and eighteen Years afterwards, *Scipio Nasica*, produced to them an Invention for measuring the Hours in cloudy Weather, it was by the Dropping of Water out of one Vessel into another, somewhat like our Sand-Glasses. Clocks and Watches, to shew the Hour, are very modern Inventions. The Sub-dividing Hours into Minutes, and Minutes into Seconds, by those curious Machines, is not older than the Days of our Fathers, but now brought to a surprising Nicety.

Since our Time is reduced to a Standard, and the Bullion of the Day minted out into Hours, the Industrious know how to employ every Piece of Time to a real Advantage in their different Professions: And he that is prodigal of his Hours, is, in Effect, a Squanderer of Money. I remember a notable Woman, who was fully sensible of the intrinsic Value of *Time*. Her Husband was a Shoemaker, and an excellent Craftsman, but never minded how the Minutes passed. In vain did she inculcate to him, That *Time is Money*. He had too much Wit to apprehend her, and it prov'd his Ruin. When at the Alehouse among his idle Companions, if one remark'd that the Clock struck Eleven, *What is that,* says he, *among us all?* If she sent him Word by the Boy, that it had struck Twelve; *Tell her to be easy, it can never be more.* If, that it had struck One, *Bid her be comforted, for it can never be less.*

If we lose our Money, it gives us some Concern. If we are cheated or robb'd of it, we are angry: But Money lost may be found; what we are robb'd of may be restored: The Treasure of Time once lost, can never be recovered; yet we squander it as tho' 'twere nothing worth, or we had no Use for it.

—*Poor Richard Improved* (1751)

116   BENJAMIN FRANKLIN

Rattle-Snakes for Felons, "Rattle-Snakes seem the most suitable Returns for the Human Serpents sent by our Mother Country" (May 9, 1751)

To the Printers of the *Gazette*:

By a Passage in one of your late Papers, I understand that the Government at home will not suffer our mistaken Assemblies to make any Law for preventing or discouraging the Importation of Convicts from Great Britain, for this kind Reason, *"That such Laws are against the Publick Utility, as they tend to prevent the* IMPROVEMENT *and* WELL PEOPLING of the Colonies."

Such a tender *parental* Concern in our *Mother Country* for the *Welfare* of her Children, calls aloud for the highest *Returns* of Gratitude and Duty. This every one must be sensible of: But 'tis said, that in our present Circumstances it is absolutely impossible for us to make *such* as are adequate to the Favour. I own it; but nevertheless let us do our Endeavour. 'Tis something to show a grateful Disposition.

In some of the uninhabited Parts of these Provinces, there are Numbers of these venomous Reptiles we call RATTLE-SNAKES; Felons-convict from the Beginning of the World: These, whenever we meet with them, we put to Death, by Virtue of an old Law, *Thou shalt bruise his Head.*

But as this is a sanguinary Law, and may seem too cruel; and as however mischievous those Creatures are with us, they may possibly change their Natures, if they were to change the Climate; I would humbly propose, that this general Sentence of Death be changed for *Transportation*.

In the Spring of the Year, when they first creep out of their Holes, they are feeble, heavy, slow, and easily taken; and if a small Bounty were allow'd *per* Head, some Thousands might be collected annually, and *transported* to Britain. There I would propose to have them carefully distributed in *St. James's Park*, in the Spring-Gardens and other Places of Pleasure about *London*; in the Gardens of all the Nobility and Gentry throughout the Nation; but particularly in the Gardens of the *Prime Ministers*, the *Lords of Trade* and *Members of Parliament*; for to them we are *most particularly* obliged.

There is no human Scheme so perfect, but some Inconveniencies may be objected to it: Yet when the Conveniences far exceed, the Scheme is judg'd rational, and fit to be executed. Thus Inconveniencies have been objected to that *good* and *wise* Act of Parliament, by virtue of which all the *Newgates* and *Dungeons* in Britain are emptied into the Colonies. It has been said, that these Thieves and Villains introduc'd among us, spoil the Morals of Youth in the Neighbourhoods that entertain them, and perpetrate many horrid Crimes: But let not *private Interests* obstruct *pub-*

lick Utility. Our *Mother* knows what is best for us. What is a little House-breaking, *Shoplifting*, or *Highway Robbing*; what is a *Son* now and then *corrupted* and *hang'd*, a Daughter *debauch'd* and pox'd, a Wife *stabb'd*, a Husband's *Throat cut*, or a Child's Brains beat out with an Axe, compar'd with this "IMPROVEMENT and WELL PEOPLING of the Colonies!"

Thus it may perhaps be objected to my Scheme, that the Rattle-Snake is a mischievous Creature, and that his changing his Nature with the Clime is a mere Supposition, not yet confirm'd by sufficient Facts. What then? Is not Example more prevalent than Precept? And may not the honest rough British Gentry, by a Familiarity with these Reptiles, learn to *creep*, and to insinuate, and to *slaver*, and to *wriggle* into Place (and perhaps to *poison* such as stand in their Way) Qualities of no small Advantage to Courtiers! In comparison of which *Improvement* and Publick Utility, what is a *Child* now and then kill'd by their venomous Bite,—or even a favourite *Lap-Dog*?

I would only add, That this Exporting of Felons to the Colonies, may be consider'd as a *Trade*, as well as in the Light of a *Favour*. Now all Commerce implies *Returns*: Justice requires them: There can be no Trade without them. And *Rattle-Snakes* seem the most *suitable Returns* for the *Human Serpents* sent by our Mother Country. In this, however, as in every other branch of trade, she will have the Advantage of us. She will reap *equal* Benefits without equal Risque of the Inconveniencies and Dangers. For the *Rattle-Snake* gives Warning before he attempts his Mischief; which the Convict does not. I am

> Yours, &c.,
> *Americanus*

> —*The Pennsylvania Gazette*

Poor Richard's Sayings for 1752

If Man could have Half his Wishes, he would double his Troubles.

The busy Man has few idle Visitors; to the boiling Pot the Flies come not.

Mankind are very odd Creatures: One Half censure what they practise, the other half practise what they censure; the rest always say and do as they ought.

For want of a Nail the Shoe is lost; for want of a Shoe the Horse is lost; for want of a Horse the Rider is lost.

Poor Richard's Sayings for 1753

Ignorance leads Men into a Party, and *Shame* keeps them from getting out again.

Sudden Power is apt to be insolent, *Sudden Liberty* saucy; that behaves best which has grown gradually.

He that is of Opinion Money will do every Thing, may well be suspected of doing every Thing for Money.

༄

Letter to Peter Collinson, "Whenever we attempt to mend the scheme of Providence" (May 9, 1753)

Sir—

I received your Favour of the 29th August last and thank you for the kind and judicious remarks you have made on my little Piece. Whatever further occurs to you on the same subject, you will much oblige me in communicating it.

I have often observed with wonder, that Temper of the poor English Manufacturers and day Labourers which you mention, and acknowledge it to be pretty general. When any of them happen to come here, where Labour is much better paid than in England, their Industry seems to diminish in equal proportion. But it is not so with the German Labourers; They retain the habitual Industry and Frugality they bring with them, and now receiving higher Wages an accumulation arises that makes them all rich.

When I consider, that the English are the Offspring of Germans, that the Climate they live in is much of the same Temperature; when I can see nothing in Nature that should create this Difference, I am apt to suspect it must arise from Institution, and I have sometimes doubted, whether the Laws peculiar to England which compel the Rich to maintain the Poor, have not given the latter, a Dependance that very much lessens the care of providing against the wants of old Age.

I have heard it remarked that the Poor in Protestant Countries on the Continent of Europe, are generally more industrious than those of Popish Countries, may not the more numerous foundations in the latter for the relief of the poor have some effect towards rendering them less provident. To relieve the misfortunes of our fellow creatures is concurring with the Deity, 'tis Godlike, but if we provide encouragements for Laziness, and supports for Folly, may it not be found fighting against the order of God and Nature, which perhaps has appointed Want and Misery as the proper Punishments for, and Cautions against as well as necessary consequences of Idleness and Extravagancy.

Whenever we attempt to mend the scheme of Providence and to interfere in the Government of the World, we had need be very circumspect lest we do more harm than Good. In New England they once thought Black-birds useless and mischievous to their corn, they made Laws to destroy them, the consequence was, the Black-birds were diminished but a kind of Worms which devoured their Grass, and which the Black-birds had been used to feed on encreased prodigiously; Then finding their Loss in Grass much greater than their saving in corn they wished again for their Black-birds.

We had here some years since a Transylvanian Tartar, who had travelled much in the East, and came hither merely to see the West, intending to go home thro' the Spanish West Indies, China &c. He asked me one day what I thought might be the Reason that so many and such numerous nations, as the Tartars in Europe and Asia, the Indians in America, and the Negroes in Africa, continued a wandring careless Life, and refused to live in Cities, and to cultivate the arts they saw practiced by the civilized part of Mankind. While I was considering what answer to make him; *I'll tell you,* says he in his broken English, *God make man for Paradise, he make him for to live lazy; man make God angry, God turn him out of Paradise, and bid him work; man no love work; he want to go to Paradise again, he want to live lazy; so all mankind love lazy.* Howe'er this may be it seems certain, that the hope of becoming at some time of Life free from the necessity of care and Labour, together with fear of penury, are the main-springs of most people's industry.

To those indeed who have been educated in elegant plenty, even the provision made for the poor may appear misery, but to those who have scarce ever been better provided for, such provision may seem quite good and sufficient, these latter have then nothing to fear worse than their present Conditions, and scarce hope for any thing better than a Parish maintainance; so that there is only the difficulty of getting that maintainance allowed while they are able to work, or a little shame they suppose attending it, that can induce them to work at all, and what they do will only be from hand to mouth.

The proneness of human Nature to a life of ease, of freedom from care and labour appears strongly in the little success that has hitherto attended every attempt to civilize our American Indians, in their present way of living, almost all their Wants are supplied by the spontaneous Productions of Nature, with the addition of very little labour, if hunting and fishing may indeed be called labour when Game is so plenty, they visit us frequently, and see the advantages that Arts, Sciences, and compact Society procure us, they are not deficient in natural understanding and yet they have never shewn any Inclination to change their manner of life for ours, or to learn any of our Arts; When an Indian Child has been brought up among us, taught our language and habituated to our Customs, yet if he goes to see his relations and make one Indian Ramble with them, there is no perswading him ever to return, and that this is not natural to them merely as Indians, but as men, is plain from this, that when white persons of either sex have been taken prisoners young by the Indians, and lived a while among them, tho' ransomed by their Friends, and treated with all imaginable tenderness to prevail with them to stay among the English, yet in a Short time they become disgusted with our manner of life, and the care and pains that are necessary to support it, and take the first good Opportunity of escaping again into the Woods, from whence there is no reclaiming them. One instance I remember to have heard, where the person was brought home to possess a good Estate; but finding some care necessary to keep it together, he relinquished it to a younger Brother, reserving to himself nothing but a gun and a match-Coat, with which he took his way again to the Wilderness.

Though they have few but natural wants and those easily supplied. But with us are infinite Artificial wants, no less craving than those of Nature, and much more difficult to satisfy; so that I am apt to imagine that close Societies subsisting by Labour and Arts, arose first not from choice, but from necessity: When numbers being driven by war from their hunting grounds and prevented by seas or by other nations were crowded together into some narrow Territories, which without labour would not afford them Food. However as matters now stand with us, care and industry seem absolutely necessary to our well being; they should therefore have every Encouragement we can invent, and not one Motive to diligence be subtracted, and the support of the Poor should not be by maintaining them in Idleness, But by employing them in some kind of labour suited to their Abilities of body &c. as I am informed of late begins to be the practice in many parts of England, where work houses are erected for that purpose. If these were general I should think the Poor would be more careful and work voluntarily and lay up something for themselves against a rainy day, rather than run the risque of being obliged to work at the pleasure of others for a bare subsistence and that too under confinement. The little value Indians set on what we prize so highly under the name of Learning appears from a pleasant passage that happened some years since at a Treaty between one of our Colonies and the Six Nations; when every thing had been settled to the Satisfaction of both sides, and nothing remained but a mutual exchange of civilities, the English Commissioners told the Indians, they had in their Country a College for the instruction of Youth who were there taught various languages, Arts, and Sciences; that there was a particular foundation in favour of the Indians to defray the expense of the Education of any of their sons who should desire to take the Benefit of it. And now if the Indians would accept of the Offer, the English would take half a dozen of their brightest lads and bring them up in the Best manner; The Indians after consulting on the proposal replied that it was remembered some of their Youths had formerly been educated in that College, but it had been observed that for a long time after they returned to their Friends, they were absolutely good for nothing being neither acquainted with the true methods of killing deer, catching Beaver or surprizing an enemy. The Proposition however, they looked on as a mark of the kindness and good will of the English to the Indian Nations which merited a grateful return; and therefore if the English Gentlemen would send a dozen or two of their Children to Onondago the great Council would take care of their Education, bring them up in really what was the best manner and make men of them.

I am perfectly of your mind, that measures of great Temper are necessary with the Germans: and am not without Apprehensions, that thro' their indiscretion or Ours, or both, great disorders and inconveniences may one day arise among us; Those who come hither are generally of the most ignorant Stupid Sort of their own Nation, and as Ignorance is often attended with Credulity when Knavery would mislead it, and with Suspicion when Honesty would set it right; and as few of the English understand the German Language, and so cannot address them either from the Press or Pulpit, 'tis almost impossible to remove any prejudices they once entertain. Their own Clergy have very little influence over the people; who seem to take an uncommon pleasure in abusing and discharging the Minister on every trivial occasion. Not being used to Liberty, they know not how to make a modest use of it; and as Kolben says of the young Hottentots, that they are not esteemed men till they have shewn their manhood by beating their mothers, so these seem to think themselves not free, till they can feel their liberty in abusing and insulting their Teachers. Thus they are under no restraint of Ecclesiastical Government; They behave, however, submissively enough at present to the Civil Government which I wish they may continue to do: For I remember when they modestly declined intermeddling in our Elections, but now they come in droves, and carry all before them, except in one or two Counties; Few of their children in the Country learn English; they import many Books from Germany; and of the six printing houses in the Province, two are entirely German, two half German half English, and but two entirely English; They have one German News-paper, and one half German.

Advertisements intended to be general are now printed in Dutch and English; the Signs in our Streets have inscriptions in both languages, and in some places only German: They begin of late to make all their Bonds and other legal Writings in their own Language, which (though I think it ought not to be) are allowed good in our Courts, where the German Business so encreases that there is continual need of Interpreters; and I suppose in a few years they will be also necessary in the Assembly, to tell one half of our Legislators what the other half say; In short unless the stream of their importation could be turned from this to other colonies, as you very judiciously propose, they will soon so out number us, that all the advantages we have will not in My Opinion be able to preserve our language, and even our Government will become precarious. The French who watch all advantages, are now themselves making a German settlement back of us in the Ilinoes Country, and by means of those Germans they may in time come to an understanding with ours, and indeed in the last war our Germans shewed a general disposition that seems to bode us no good; for when the English who were not Quakers, alarmed by the danger arising from the defenceless state of our Country entered unanimously into an Association within this Government and the lower Countries raised armed and Disciplined near 10,000 men, the Germans except a very few in proportion to their numbers refused to engage in it, giving out one among another, and even in print, that if they were quiet the French should they take the Country would not molest them; at the same time abusing the Philadelphians for fitting out Privateers against the Enemy; and representing the trouble hazard and Expence of defending the Province, as a greater inconvenience than any that might be expected from a change of Government. Yet I am not for refusing entirely to admit them into our Colonies: all that seems to be necessary is, to distribute them more equally, mix them with the English, establish English Schools where they are now too thick settled, and take some care to prevent the practice lately fallen into by some of the Ship Owners, of sweeping the German Gaols to make up the number of their Passengers. I say I am not against the Admission of Germans in general, for they have their Virtues, their industry and frugality is exemplary; They are excellent husbandmen and contribute greatly to the improvement of a Country.

I pray God long to preserve to Great Britain the English Laws, Manners, Liberties and Religion notwithstanding the complaints so frequent in Your public papers, of the prevailing corruption and degeneracy of your People; I know you have a great deal of Virtue still subsisting among you, and I hope the Constitution is not so near a dissolution, as some seem to apprehend; I do not think you are generally become such Slaves to your Vices, as to draw down that Justice Milton speaks of when he says that

  —sometimes Nations will descend so low
From reason, which is virtue, that no Wrong,
But Justice, and some fatal curse annex'd
Deprives them of their outward liberty,
Their inward lost.
      —*Paradise Lost*

In history we find that Piety, Public Spirit and military Prowess have their Flows, as well as their ebbs, in every nation, and that the Tide is never so low but it may rise again; But should this dreaded fatal change happen in my time, how should I even in the midst of the Affliction rejoice, if we have been able to preserve those invaluable treasures, and can invite the good among you to come and partake of them! O let not Britain seek to oppress us, but like an affectionate parent endeavour to secure freedom to her children; they may be able one day to assist her in defending her own—Whereas a Mortification begun in the Foot may spread upwards to the destruction of the nobler parts of the Body.

I fear I have already extended this rambling letter beyond your patience, and therefore conclude with requesting your acceptance of the inclosed Pamphlet from Sir Your most humble servant

              —Writings

Poor Richard's Sayings for 1754

Love your Neighbour; yet don't pull down your Hedge.

The learned Fool writes his Nonsense in better Language than the unlearned; but still 'tis Nonsense.

Praise little, dispraise less.

Poor Richard's Sayings for 1755

Diligence overcomes Difficulties, Sloth makes them.

A long Life may not be good enough, but a good Life is long enough.

Be at War with your Vices, at Peace with your Neighbours, and let every New-Year find you a better Man.

Where there is Hunger, Law is not regarded; and where Law is not regarded, there will be Hunger.

The Wolf sheds his Coat once a Year, his Disposition never.

Being ignorant is not so much a Shame, as being unwilling to learn.

The Doors of Wisdom are never shut.

Who is wise? He that learns from every One.
Who is powerful? He that governs his Passions.
Who is rich? He that is content.
Who is that? Nobody.

※

From his *Autobiography*, "When Men are employ'd" (c. Winter 1755–1756)

...when Men are employ'd they are best contented. For on the Days they work'd they were good-natur'd and cheerful; and with the consciousness of having done a good Day's work they spent the Evenings jollily; but on the idle Days they were mutinous and quarrelsome, finding fault with their Pork, the Bread, &c. and in continual ill-humor; which put me in mind of a Sea-Captain, whose Rule it was to keep his Men constantly at Work; and when his Mate once told him that they had done every thing, and there was nothing farther to employ them about; O, says he, *make them scour the Anchor.*

—*The Autobiography,* Part 3

※

Poor Richard's Sayings for 1756

Laziness travels so slowly, that *Poverty* soon overtakes him.

Be civil to all; serviceable to many; familiar with few; Friend to one; Enemy to none.

Laws too gentle are seldom obeyed; too severe, seldom executed.

Love your Enemies, for they tell you your Faults.

~

Poor Richard's Sayings for 1757

Work as if you were to live 100 Years, Pray as if you were to die To-morrow.

Men take more pains to mask than mend.

It is Ill-Manners to silence a Fool, and Cruelty to let him go on.

~

Homily, "To be content"

Some antient Philosophers have said, that Happiness depends more on the inward Disposition of Mind than on outward Circumstances; and that he who cannot be happy in any State, can be so in no State. To be happy, they tell us we must be content. Right. But they do not teach how we may become content. *Poor Richard* shall give you a short good Rule for that. *To be content, look backward on those who possess less than yourself, not forward on those who possess more.* If this does not make you content, you don't deserve to be *happy*.

—*Poor Richard Improved*, 1757

༈

Poor Richard's Preface, 1758, a.k.a. "The Way to Wealth" or "Father Abraham's Speech"

Courteous Reader,

I have heard that nothing gives an Author so great Pleasure, as to find his Works respectfully quoted by other learned Authors. This Pleasure I have seldom enjoyed; for tho' I have been, if I may say it without Vanity, an *eminent Author* of Almanacks annually now a full Quarter of a Century, my Brother Authors in the same Way, for what Reason I know not, have ever been very sparing in their Applauses; and no other Author has taken the least Notice of me, so that did not my Writings produce me some solid

Pudding, the great Deficiency of *Praise* would have quite discouraged me.

I concluded at length, that the People were the best Judges of my Merit; for they buy my Works; and besides, in my Rambles, where I am not personally known, I have frequently heard one or other of my Adages repeated, with, *as Poor Richard says*, at the End on't; this gave me some Satisfaction, as it showed not only that my Instructions were regarded, but discovered likewise some Respect for my Authority; and I own, that to encourage the Practice of remembering and repeating those wise Sentences, I have sometimes *quoted myself* with great Gravity.

Judge then how much I must have been gratified by an Incident I am going to relate to you. I stopt my Horse lately where a great Number of People were collected at a Vendue of Merchant Goods. The Hour of Sale not being come, they were conversing on the Badness of the Times, and one of the Company call'd to a plain clean old Man, with white Locks, *Pray, Father* Abraham, *what think you of the Times? Won't these heavy Taxes quite ruin the Country? How shall we be ever able to pay them? What would you advise us to?*—Father *Abraham* stood up, and reply'd, If you'd have my Advice, I'll give it you in short, for a *Word to the Wise is enough*, and *many Words won't fill a Bushel*, as *Poor Richard* says. They join'd in desiring him to speak his Mind, and gathering round him, he proceeded as follows:

Friends, says he, and Neighbours, the Taxes are indeed very heavy, and if those laid on by the Government were the only Ones we had to pay, we might more easily discharge them; but we have many others, and much more grievous to some of us. We are taxed twice as much by our *Idleness*, three times as much by our *Pride*, and four times as much by our *Folly*, and from these Taxes the Commissioners cannot ease or deliver us by allowing an Abatement. However let us hearken to good Advice, and something may be done for us; *God helps them that help themselves*, as *Poor Richard says,* in his Almanack of 1733.

....

So what signifies *wishing* and *hoping* for better Times. We may make these Times better if we bestir ourselves. *Industry need not wish*, as *Poor Richard* says, and *He that lives upon Hope will die fasting. There are no Gains, without Pains;* then *Help Hands, for I have no Lands*, or if I have, they are smartly taxed. And, as *Poor Richard* likewise observes, *He that hath a Trade hath an Estate*, and *He that hath a Calling hath an Office of Profit and Honour;* but then the *Trade* must be worked at, and the *Calling* well followed, or neither the *Estate*, nor the *Office*, will enable us to pay our Taxes.—If we are industrious we shall never starve; for, as *Poor Richard* says, *At the working Man's House* Hunger *looks in, but dares not enter.* Nor will the Bailiff or the Constable enter, for *Industry pays Debts, while Despair encreaseth them*, says *Poor Richard.*—What though you have found no Treasure, nor has any rich Relation left you a Legacy, *Diligence is the Mother of Good-luck,* as *Poor Richard* says, and *God gives all Things to Industry.* Then *plough deep, while Sluggards sleep, and you shall have Corn to sell and to keep,* says *Poor Dick.* Work while it is called To-day, for you know not how much you may be hindered To-morrow, which makes *Poor Richard* say, *One To-day is worth two To-morrows;* and farther, *Have you somewhat to do To-morrow, do it To-day.* If you were a Servant, would you not be ashamed that a good Master should catch you idle? Are you then your own Master, *be ashamed to catch yourself idle,* as *Poor Dick* says. When there is so much to be done for yourself, your Family, your Country, and your gracious King, be up by Peep of Day; *Let not the Sun look down and say, Inglorious here he lies.* Handle your Tools without Mittens; remember that *the Cat in Gloves catches no Mice,* as *Poor Richard* says. 'Tis true there is much to be done, and perhaps you are weak handed, but stick to it steadily, and you will see great Effects, for *constant Dropping wears away Stones,* and by *Diligence and Patience the Mouse ate in two the Cable;* and *little Strokes fell great Oaks,* as *Poor Richard* says in his Almanack, the Year I cannot just now remember.

Methinks I hear some of you say, *Must a Man afford himself no Leisure?*—I will tell thee, my Friend, what *Poor Richard* says, *Employ thy Time well if thou meanest to gain Leisure;* and, *since thou art not sure of a Minute, throw not away an Hour.* Leisure, is Time for doing something useful; this Leisure the diligent Man will obtain, but the lazy Man never; so that, as *Poor Richard* says, a *Life of Leisure and a Life of Laziness are two Things.* Do you imagine that Sloth will afford you more Comfort than Labour? No, for as *Poor Richard* says, *Trouble springs from Idleness, and grievous Toil from needless Ease. Many without Labour, would live by their* Wits *only, but they break for want of Stock.* Whereas Industry gives Comfort, and Plenty, and Respect: *Fly Pleasures, and they'll follow you. The diligent Spinner has a large Shift;* and *now I have a Sheep and a Cow, every Body bids me Good morrow;* all which is well said by *Poor Richard.*

But with our Industry, we must likewise be *steady, settled* and *careful,* and oversee our own Affairs *with our own Eyes,* and not trust too much to others; for, as *Poor Richard says,*

> *I never saw an oft removed Tree,*
> *Nor yet an oft removed Family,*
> *That throve so well as those that settled be.*

And again, *Three Removes is as bad as a Fire;* and again, *Keep thy Shop, and thy Shop will keep thee;* and again, *If you would have your Business done, go; If not, send.* And again,

> *He that by the Plough would thrive,*
> *Himself must either hold or drive.*

And again, *The Eye of a Master will do more Work than both his Hands;* and again, *Want of Care does us more Damage than Want of Knowledge;* and again, *Not to oversee Workmen, is to leave them your Purse open.* Trusting too much to others Care is the Ruin of many; for, as the *Almanack* says, *In the Affairs of this World, Men are saved, not by Faith, but by the Want of it;* but a Man's own Care is profitable; for, saith *Poor Dick, Learning is to the Studious*, and *Riches to the Careful*, as well as *Power to the Bold*, and *Heaven to the Virtuous.* And farther, *If you would have a faithful Servant, and one that you like, serve yourself.* And again, he adviseth to Circumspection and Care, even in the smallest Matters, because sometimes *a little Neglect may breed great Mischief;* adding, *For want of a Nail the Shoe was lost; for want of a Shoe the Horse was lost; and for want of a Horse the Rider was lost*, being overtaken and slain by the Enemy, all for want of Care about a Horse-shoe Nail.

So much for Industry, my Friends, and Attention to one's own Business; but to these we must add *Frugality*, if we would make our *Industry* more certainly successful. A Man may, if he knows not how to save as he gets, *keep his Nose all his Life to the Grindstone*, and die not worth a *Groat* at last. *A fat Kitchen makes a lean Will,* as *Poor Richard* says; and,

> *Many Estates are spent in the Getting,*
> *Since Women for Tea forsook Spinning and Knitting,*
> *And Men for Punch forsook Hewing and Splitting.*

If you would be wealthy, says he, in another Almanack, *think of Saving as well as of Getting:* The Indies *have not made* Spain *rich, because her* Outgoes *are greater than her* Incomes. Away then with your expensive Follies, and you will not have so much Cause to complain of hard Times, heavy Taxes, and chargeable Families; for, as *Poor Dick* says,

> *Women and Wine, Game and Deceit,*
> *Make the Wealth small, and the Wants great.*

And farther, *What maintains one Vice, would bring up two Children.* You may think perhaps, That a *little* Tea, or a *little* Punch now and then, Diet a *little* more costly, Clothes a *little* finer, and a *little* Entertainment now and then, can be no *great* Matter; but remember what *Poor Richard* says, *Many* a Little *makes a Mickle;* and farther, *Beware of* little *Expences; a small Leak will sink a great Ship;* and again, *Who Dainties love, shall Beggars prove;* and moreover, *Fools make Feasts, and wise Men eat them.*

Here you are all got together at this Vendue of *Fineries* and *Knicknacks.* You call them *Goods,* but if you do not take Care, they will prove *Evils* to some of you. You expect they will be sold *cheap*, and perhaps they may for less than they cost; but if you have no Occasion for them, they must be *dear* to you. Remember what *Poor Richard* says, *Buy what thou hast no Need of, and ere long thou shalt sell thy Necessaries.* And again, *At a great Pennyworth pause a while:* He means, that perhaps the Cheapness is *apparent* only, and not *real;* or the Bargain, by straitning thee in thy Business, may do thee more Harm than Good. For in another Place he says, *Many have been ruined by buying good Pennyworths.* Again, *Poor Richard* says, *'Tis foolish to lay out Money in a Purchase of Repentance;* and yet this Folly is practised every Day at Vendues, for want of minding the Almanack. *Wise Men*, as *Poor Dick* says, *learn by others Harms, Fools scarcely by their own;* but, *Felix quem faciunt aliena Pericula cautum*[6]. Many a one, for the Sake of Finery on the Back, have gone with a hungry Belly, and half starved their Families; *Silks and Sattins, Scarlet and Velvets,* as *Poor Richard* says, *put out the Kitchen Fire.* These are not the *Necessaries* of Life; they can scarcely be called the *Conveniencies,* and yet only because they look pretty, how many *want* to *have* them. The *artificial* Wants of Mankind thus become more numerous than the *natural;* and, as *Poor Dick* says, *For one* poor *Person, there are an hundred* indigent. By these, and other Extravagancies, the Genteel are reduced to Poverty, and forced

---

6   happy are those who learn from others' troubles

to borrow of those whom they formerly despised, but who through *Industry* and *Frugality* have maintained their Standing; in which Case it appears plainly, that a *Ploughman on his Legs is higher than a Gentleman on his Knees*, as *Poor Richard* says. Perhaps they have had a small Estate left them, which they knew not the Getting of; they think *'tis Day, and will never be Night*; that a little to be spent out of *so much*, is not worth minding; *(a Child and a Fool,* as *Poor Richard* says, *imagine* Twenty Shillings *and Twenty Years can never be spent)* but, *always taking out of the Meal-tub, and never putting in, soon comes to the Bottom;* then, as *Poor Dick* says, *When the Well's dry, they know the Worth of Water.* But this they might have known before, if they had taken his Advice; *If you would know the Value of Money, go and try to borrow some* for, *he that goes a borrowing goes a sorrowing;* and indeed so does he that lends to such People, when he goes *to get it in again.*—*Poor Dick* farther advises, and says,

> *Fond* Pride of Dress, *is sure a very Curse;*
> *E'er* Fancy *you consult, consult your Purse.*

And again, *Pride is as loud a Beggar as Want, and a great deal more saucy.* When you have bought one fine Thing you must buy ten more, that your Appearance may be all of a Piece; but *Poor Dick* says, *'Tis easier* to suppress *the first Desire, than to* satisfy *all that follow it.* And 'tis as truly Folly for the Poor to ape the Rich, as for the Frog to swell, in order to equal the Ox.

> *Great Estates may venture more,*
> *But little Boats should keep near Shore.*

'Tis however a Folly soon punished; for *Pride that dines on Vanity sups on Contempt*, as *Poor Richard* says. And in another Place, *Pride breakfasted with Plenty, dined with Poverty, and supped with Infamy*. And after all, of what Use is this *Pride of Appearance*, for which so much is risked, so much is suffered? It cannot promote Health, or ease Pain; it makes no Increase of Merit in the Person, it creates Envy, it hastens Misfortune.

> *What is a Butterfly? At best*
> *He's but a Caterpillar drest*
> *The gaudy Fop's his Picture just,*

as *Poor Richard* says.

But what Madness must it be to *run in Debt* for these Superfluities! We are offered, by the Terms of this Vendue, *Six Months Credit;* and that perhaps has induced some of us to attend it, because we cannot spare the ready Money, and hope now to be fine without it. But, ah, think what you do when you run in Debt; *You give to another Power over your Liberty.* If you cannot pay at the Time, you will be ashamed to see your Creditor; you will be in Fear when you speak to him; you will make poor pitiful sneaking Excuses, and by Degrees come to lose your Veracity, and sink into base down right lying; for, as *Poor Richard* says, *The second Vice is Lying, the first is running in Debt.* And again, to the same Purpose, *Lying rides upon Debt's Back.* Whereas a freeborn *Englishman* ought not to be ashamed or afraid to see or speak to any Man living. But Poverty often deprives a Man of all Spirit and Virtue: *'Tis hard for an empty Bag to stand upright,* as *Poor Richard* truly says. What would you think of that Prince, or that Government, who should issue an Edict forbidding you to dress like a Gentleman or a Gentlewoman, on Pain of Imprisonment or Servitude? Would you not say, that you are free, have a Right to dress as you please, and that such an Edict would be a Breach of your Privileges, and such a Government tyrannical? And yet you are about to put yourself under that Tyranny when you run in Debt for such Dress! Your Creditor has Authority at his Pleasure to deprive you of your Liberty, by confining you in Gaol for Life, or to sell you for a Servant, if you should not be able to pay him! When you have got your Bargain, you may, perhaps, think little of Payment; but *Creditors, Poor Richard* tells us, *have better Memories than Debtors;* and in another Place says, *Creditors are a superstitious Sect, great Observers of set Days and Times.* The Day comes round before you are aware, and the Demand is made before you are prepared to satisfy it. Or if you bear your Debt in Mind, the Term which at first seemed so long, will, as it lessens, appear extreamly short. *Time* will seem to have added Wings to his Heels as well as Shoulders. *Those have a short Lent,* saith *Poor Richard, who owe Money to be paid at Easter.* Then since, as he says, *The Borrower is a Slave to the Lender, and the Debtor to the Creditor*, disdain the Chain, preserve your Freedom; and maintain your Independency: Be *industrious* and *free;* be *frugal* and *free.* At present, perhaps, you may think yourself in thriving Circumstances, and that you can bear a little Extravagance without Injury; but,

> For Age and Want, save while you may;
> No Morning Sun lasts a whole Day,

as *Poor Richard* says.—Gain may be temporary and uncertain, but ever while you live, Expence is constant and certain; and *'tis easier to build two Chimnies than to keep one in Fuel,* as *Poor Richard* says. So *rather go to Bed supperless than rise in Debt.*

> Get what you can, and what you get hold;
> 'Tis the Stone that will turn all your Lead into Gold,

as *Poor Richard* says. And when you have got the Philosopher's Stone, sure you will no longer complain of bad Times, or the Difficulty of paying Taxes.

This Doctrine, my Friends, is *Reason* and *Wisdom* ; but after all, do not depend too much upon your own *Industry*, and *Frugality*, and *Prudence*, though excellent Things, for they may all be blasted without the Blessing of Heaven; and therefore ask that Blessing humbly, and be not uncharitable to those that at present seem to want it, but comfort and help them. Remember *Job* suffered, and was afterwards prosperous.

And now to conclude, *Experience keeps a dear School, but Fools will learn in no other, and scarce in that;* for it is true, *we may give Advice, but we cannot give Conduct,* as *Poor Richard* says: However, remember this, *They that won't be counselled, can't be helped,* as *Poor Richard* says: And farther, That *if you will not hear Reason, she'll surely rap your Knuckles.*

Thus the old Gentleman ended his Harangue. The People heard it, and approved the Doctrine, and immediately practised the contrary, just as if it had been a common Sermon; for the Vendue opened, and they began to buy extravagantly, notwithstanding all his Cautions, and their own Fear of Taxes.—I found the good Man had thoroughly studied my Almanacks, and digested all I had dropt on those Topicks during the Course of Five-and-twenty Years. The frequent Mention he made of me must have tired any one else, but my Vanity was wonderfully delighted with it, though I was conscious that not a tenth Part of the Wisdom was my own which he ascribed to me, but rather the

Gleanings I had made of the Sense of all Ages and Nations. However, I resolved to be the better for the Echo of it; and though I had at first determined to buy Stuff for a new Coat, I went away resolved to wear my old One a little longer. *Reader*, if thou wilt do the same, thy Profit will be as great as mine.

I am, as ever,
Thine to serve thee,
RICHARD SAUNDERS

July 7, 1757

ॐ

Poor Richard's Sayings for 1758

Silence is not always a Sign of Wisdom, but Babbling is ever a Mark of Folly.

Virtue may not always make a Face handsome, but *Vice* will certainly make it ugly.

Great Modesty often hides great Merit.

Fools need Advice most, but wise Men only are the better for it.

Half the Truth is often a great Lie.

Letter to John Baskerville, "the Prejudice some have entertained against Your Work" (c. 1760)

Dear Sir,

Let me give you a pleasant Instance of the Prejudice some have entertained against your Work. Soon after I returned, discoursing with a Gentleman concerning the Artists of Birmingham, he said you would be a Means of blinding all the Readers in the Nation, for the Strokes of your Letters being too thin and narrow, hurt the Eye, and he could never read a Line of them without Pain. I thought, said I, you were going to complain of the Gloss on the Paper, some object to: No, no, says he, I have heard that mentioned, but it is not that; 'tis in the Form and Cut of the Letters themselves; they have not that natural and easy Proportion between the Height and Thickness of the Stroke, which makes the common Printing so much more comfortable to the Eye.—You see this Gentleman was a Connoisseur. In vain I endeavoured to support your Character against the Charge; he knew what he felt, he could see the Reason of it, and several other Gentlemen among his Friends had made the same Observation, &c.

Yesterday he called to visit me, when, mischievously bent to try his Judgment, I stept into my Closet, tore off the Top of Mr. Caslon's Speci-

men, and produced it to him as yours brought with me from Birmingham, saying, I had been examining it since he spoke to me, and could not for my Life perceive the Disproportion he mentioned, desiring him to point it out to me. He readily undertook it, and went over the several Fonts, shewing me every-where what he thought Instances of that Disproportion; and declared, that he could not then read the Specimen without feeling very strongly the Pain he had mentioned to me. I spared him that Time the Confusion of being told, that these were the Types he had been reading all his Life with so much Ease to his Eyes; the Types his adored Newton is printed with, on which he has pored not a little; nay, the very Types his own Book is printed with, for he is himself an Author; and yet never discovered this painful Disproportion in them, till he thought they were yours.

I am, &c.;

—Writings

Letter to David Hume, Lightning Rods and Maypoles
(May 19, 1762)

Dear Sir,

It is no small Pleasure to me to hear from you that my Paper on the means of preserving Buildings from Damage by Lightning, was acceptable to the Philosophical Society. Mr. Russel's Proposals of Improvement are very sensible and just. A Leaden Spout or Pipe is undoubtedly a good Conductor so far as it goes. If the Conductor enters the Ground just at the Foundation, and from thence is carried horizontally to some Well, or to a distant Rod driven downright into the Earth; I would then propose that the Part under Ground should be Lead, as less liable to consume with Rust than Iron. Because if the Conductor near the Foot of the Wall should be wasted, the Lightning might act on the Moisture of the Earth, and by suddenly rarifying it occasion an Explosion that may damage the Foundation. In the Experiment of discharging my large Case of Electrical Bottles thro' a Piece of small Glass Tube fill'd with Water, the suddenly rarify'd Water has exploded with a Force equal, I think, to that of so much Gunpowder; bursting the Tube into many Pieces, and driving them with Violence in all Directions and to all Parts of the Room. The Shivering of Trees into small Splinters like a Broom, is probably owing to this Rarefaction of the Sap in the longitudinal Pores or capillary Pipes in the Substance of the Wood. And the Blowing-up of Bricks or Stones in a Hearth, Rending Stones out of a Foundation, and Splitting of Walls, is also probably an Effect sometimes of rarify'd Moisture in the Earth, under the Hearth, or in the Walls. We should therefore have a durable Conductor under Ground, or convey the Lightning to the Earth at some Distance.

It must afford Lord Mareschall a good deal of Diversion to preside in a Dispute so ridiculous as that you mention. Judges in their Decisions often use Precedents. I have somewhere met with one that is what the Lawyers call a Case in Point. The Church People and the Puritans in a Country Town, had once a bitter Contention concerning the Erecting of a Maypole, which the former desir'd and the latter oppos'd. Each Party endeavour'd to strengthen itself by obtaining the Authority of the Mayor, directing or forbidding a Maypole. He heard their Altercation with great Patience, and then gravely determin'd thus; *You that are for having no Maypole shall have no Maypole; and you that are for having a Maypole shall have a Maypole. Get about your Business and let me hear no more of this Quarrel.* So methinks Lord Mareschal might say; *You that are for no more Damnation than is proportion'd to your Offences, have my Consent that it may be so: And you that are for being damn'd eternally, G——d eternally d——n you all, and let me hear no more of your Disputes.*

Your Compliment of Gold and Wisdom is very obliging to me, but a little injurious to your Country. The various Value of every thing in every Part of this World, arises you know from the various Proportions of the Quantity to the Demand. We are told that Gold and Silver in Solomon's Time were so plenty as to be of no more Value in his Country than the Stones in the Street. You have here at present just such a Plenty of Wisdom. Your People are therefore not to be censur'd for desiring no more among them than they have; and if I have any, I should certainly carry it where from its Scarcity it may probably come to a better Market.

I nevertheless regret extreamly the leaving a Country in which I have receiv'd so much Friendship, and Friends whose Conversation has been so agreable and so improving to me; and that I am henceforth to reside at so great a Distance from them is no small Mortification, to My dear Friend,

> Yours most affectionately,
> *B. FRANKLIN*

—Writings

Pax quaeitur Bello, "Peace through War" (January 26, 1766)

[When reason and appeals to self-interest failed, Franklin's political satire could take a very sharp point. The historian Edmund Morgan observes: "Only when men in power acted foolishly, adopting policies harmful to others, did he lift the restraints on both his passions and his wit."]

To the Printer of the Public Advertiser.
SIR,

The very important Controversy being next Tuesday to be finally determined between the Mother Country and their rebellious American Children, I shall think myself happy if I can furnish any Hints that may be of public Utility.

There are some Persons besides the Americans so amazingly stupid, as to distinguish in this Dispute between Power and Right, as tho' the former did not always imply the latter. The Right of Conquest invests the Conqueror with Authority to establish what Laws he pleases, however contrary to the Laws of Nature, and the common Rights of Mankind. Examine every Form of Government at this Day subsisting on the Face

---

7   Edmund S. Morgan. *Benjamin Franklin.* New Haven: Yale University Press. 2002. 36–37.

of the Globe, from the absolute Despotism of the Grand Sultan to the Democratic Government of the City of Geneva, and it will be found that the Exertion of Power in those Hands with whom it is lodged, however unconstitutional, is always justified. The Reign of the Stuarts might serve to exemplify this Observation. Happy it was for the Nation that, upon Trial, the superior Power was found to be in the People. The American Plea of Right, their Appeal to Magna Charta, must of course be set aside; and I make no Doubt but the Grand Council of the Nation will at all Hazards insist upon an absolute Submission to the Tax imposed upon them. But that they will comply without coercive Measures, is to me a Matter of very great Doubt: For when we consider, that these People, especially the more Northern Colonies, are the Descendants of your Pymms, Hampdens, and others of the like Stamp, those outrageous Assertors of Civil and Religious Liberties; that they have been nursed up in the same Old English Principles; that a little more than a Century ago their Forefathers, many of them of Family and Fortune, left their native Land, and endured all the Distresses and Hardships which are the necessary Consequences of an Establishment in a new uncultivated Country, surrounded with a cruel Blood-thirsty Enemy, oftentimes severely pinched with Cold and Hunger; and all this to enjoy unmolested that Liberty which they thought was infringed: I say, however these People may be mistaken, they will not tamely give up what they call their natural, their constitutional Rights. Force must therefore be made use of.

Now in order to bring these People to a proper Temper, I have a Plan to propose, which I think cannot fail, and which will be entirely consistent with the Oeconomy at present so much in Vogue. It is so cheap a Way of going to work, that even Mr. G— G—, that great Oeconomist, could have no reasonable Objection to it.

Let Directions be given, that Two Thousand Highlanders be immediately raised, under proper Officers of their own. It ought to be no Objection, that they were in the Rebellion in Forty-five: If Roman Catholics, the better. The C—l at present in the P—ze Service may be at their Head. Transport them early in the Spring to Quebec: There with the Canadians, natural Enemies to our Colonists, who would voluntarily engage, might make a Body of Five or Six Thousand Men; and I doubt not, by artful Management, and the Value of two or three Thousand Pounds in Presents, with the Hopes of Plunder, as likewise a Gratuity for every Scalp, the Savages on the Frontiers might be engaged to join, at least they would make a Diversion, which could not fail of being useful. I could point out a very proper General to command the Expedition; he is of a very sanguine Disposition, and has an inordinate Thirst for Fame, and besides has the Hearts of the Canadians. He might march from Canada, cross the Lakes, and fall upon these People without their expecting or being prepared for him, and with very little Difficulty over-run the whole Country.

The Business might be done without employing any of the Regular Troops quartered in the Country, and I think it would be best they should remain neuter, as it is to be feared they would be rather backward in embruing their Hands in the Blood of their Brethren and Fellow Subjects.

I would propose, that all the Capitals of the several Provinces should be burnt to the Ground, and that they cut the Throats of all the Inhabitants, Men, Women, and Children, and scalp them, to serve as an Example; that all the Shipping should be destroyed, which will effectually prevent Smuggling, and save the Expence of Guarda Costas.

No Man in his Wits, after such terrible Military Execution, will refuse to purchase stamp'd Paper. If any one should hesitate, five or six Hundred Lashes in a cold frosty Morning would soon bring him to Reason.

If the Massacre should be objected to, as it would too much depopulate the Country, it may be replied, that the Interruption this Method would occasion to Commerce, would cause so many Bankruptcies, such Numbers of Manufacturers and Labourers would be unemployed, that, together with the Felons from our Gaols, we should soon be enabled to transport such Numbers to repeople the Colonies, as to make up for any

Deficiency which Example made it necessary to sacrifice for the Public Good. Great Britain might then reign over a loyal and submissive People, and be morally certain, that no Act of Parliament would ever after be disputed.

Yours,
Pacificus
—*The Public Advertiser,* January 26, 1766

ॐ

The Stamp-Act, "a red hot Iron in his Hand" (March 23, 1767)

To the Printer—

It is reported, I know not with what Foundation, that there is an Intention of obliging the Americans to pay for all the Stamps they ought to have used, between the Commencement of the Act, and the Day on which the Repeal takes Place, *viz.* from the first of November 1765, to the first of May 1766; that this is to make Part of an Act, which is to give Validity to the Writings and Law Proceedings, that contrary to Law have been executed without Stamps, and is to be the Condition on which they are to receive that Validity. Shall we then keep up for a Trifle the Heats and Animosities that have been occasioned by the Stamp-Act? and lose all the Benefit of Harmony and good Understanding between the different Parts of the Empire, which were expected from a generous total Repeal? Is this Pittance likely to be a Whit more easily collected than the whole Duty? Where are Officers to be found who will undertake to collect it? Who is to protect them while they are about it? In my Opinion, it will meet with the same Opposition, and be attended with the same Mischiefs that would have attended an Enforcement of the Act entire.

But I hear, that this is thought necessary, to raise a Fund for defraying the Expence that has been incurred by stamping so much Paper and Parchment for the Use of America, which they have refused to take and turn'd upon our Hands; and that since they are highly favour'd by the Repeal, they cannot with any Face of Decency refuse to make good the Charges we have been at on their Account. The whole Proceeding would put one in Mind of the Frenchman that used to accost English and other Strangers on the Pont-Neuf, with many Compliments, and a red hot Iron in his Hand; *Pray Monsieur Anglois,* says he, *Do me the Favour to let me have the Honour of thrusting this hot Iron into your Backside? Zoons, what does the Fellow mean! Begone with your Iron, or I'll break your Head! Nay, Monsieur,* replies he, *if you do not chuse it, I do not insist upon it. But at least, you will in Justice have the Goodness to pay me something for the heating of my Iron.*

—*The Pennsylvania Chronicle*

New Fables (January 2, 1770)

[Franklin continued to twit the leaders of the British government who could not see how the American colonies had grown up and deserved self-representation.]

New Fables, humbly inscribed to the S—y of St—e for the American Department.

FABLE I. A Herd of Cows had long afforded Plenty of Milk, Butter and Cheese to an avaritious Farmer, who grudged them the Grass they subsisted on, and at length mowed it to make Money of the Hay, leaving them to shift for Food as they could, and yet still expected to milk them as before; but the Cows, offended with his Unreasonableness, resolved for the future to suckle one another.

FABLE II. An Eagle, King of Birds, sailing on his Wings aloft over a Farmer's Yard, saw a Cat there basking in the Sun, mistook it for a Rabbit, stoop'd, seized it, and carried it up into the Air, intending to prey on it. The Cat turning, set her Claws into the Eagle's Breast; who, finding his Mistake, opened his Talons, and would have let her drop; but Puss, unwilling to fall so far, held faster; and the Eagle, to get rid of the Inconvenience, found it necessary to set her down where he took her up.

Fable III. A Lion's Whelp was put on board a Guinea Ship bound to America as a Present to a Friend in that Country: It was tame and harmless as a Kitten, and therefore not confined, but suffered to walk about the Ship at Pleasure. A stately, full-grown English Mastiff, belonging to the Captain, despising the Weakness of the young Lion, frequently took its Food by Force, and often turned it out of its Lodging Box, when he had a Mind to repose therein himself. The young Lion nevertheless grew daily in Size and Strength, and the Voyage being long, he became at last a more equal Match for the Mastiff; who continuing his Insults, received a stunning Blow from the Lion's Paw that fetched his Skin over his Ears, and deterred him from any future Contest with such growing Strength; regretting that he had not rather secured its Friendship than provoked its Enmity.

—*The Public Advertise*

From his *Autobiography*, "living one's Life over again" (c. 1771)

...were it offer'd to my Choice, I should have no Objection to a Repetition of the same Life from its Beginning, only asking the Advantage Authors have in a second Edition to correct some Faults of the first. So would I if I might, besides correcting the Faults, change some sinister Accidents & Events of it for others more favourable, but tho' this were deny'd, I should still accept the Offer. However, since such a Repetition is not to be expected, the Thing most like living one's Life over again, seems to be a *Recollection* of that Life; and to make that Recollection as durable as possible, the putting it down in Writing.

—*The Autobiography*, Part 1

☙

From his *Autobiography*, "rambling Digressions" (c. 1771)

By my rambling Digressions I perceive my self to be grown old. I us'd to write more methodically.—But one does not dress for private Company as for a publick Ball. 'Tis perhaps only Negligence.

—*The Autobiography*, Part 1 [1771]

☙

From his *Autobiography*, "There are Croakers in every Country," (c. 1771)

There are Croakers in every Country, always boding its Ruin. Such a one then lived in Philadelphia—a person of note, an elderly man, with a wise look and a very grave manner of speaking; his name was Samuel Mickle. This gentleman, a stranger to me, stopt one day at my door, and asked me if I was the young man who had lately opened a new printing-house. Being answered in the affirmative, he said he was sorry for me, because it was an expensive undertaking, and the expense would be lost; for Philadelphia was a sinking place, the people already half bankrupts, or near being so; all appearances to the contrary, such as new buildings and the rise of rents, being to his certain knowledge fallacious, for they were, in fact, among the things that would soon ruin us. And he gave me such a detail of misfortunes now existing, or that were soon to exist, that he left me half melancholy. Had I known him before I engaged in this business, probably I never should have done it. This man continued to live in this decaying place, and to declaim in the same strain, refusing for many years to buy a house there, because all was going to destruction; and at last I had the pleasure of seeing him give five times as much for one as he might have bought it for when he first began his Croaking.

—*The Autobiography*, Part 1 [1771]

Letter to Anna Mordaunt Shipley, "what sort of Husbands would be fittest" (August 13, 1771)

[In London, Franklin was a close friend of the Bishop Jonathan Shipley and his family. Here he writes a letter to amuse Shipley's wife about the conversation he had with Kitty, the Shipleys' eleven-year-old daughter, about her older sisters' and her own marriage prospects.]

Dear Madam,

This is just to let you know that we arriv'd safe and well in Marlborough Street about Six, where I deliver'd up my Charge.

The above seems too short for a Letter; so I will lengthen it by a little Account of our Journey. The first Stage we were rather pensive. I tried several Topics of Conversation, but none of them would hold. But after Breakfast, we began to recover Spirits, and had a good deal of Chat. Will you hear some of it? We talk'd of her Brother, and she wish'd he was married. *And don't you wish your Sisters married too?* "Yes. All but Emily; I would not have her married." *Why?* "Because I can't spare her, I can't part with her. The rest may marry as soon as they please, so they do but get good Husbands."

We then took upon us to consider for 'em what sort of Husbands would be fittest for every one of them. We began with Georgiana. She thought a

Country Gentleman, that lov'd Travelling and would take her with him, that lov'd Books and would hear her read to him; I added, *that had a good Estate and was a Member of Parliament and lov'd to see an Experiment now and then.* This she agreed to; so we set him down for Georgiana, and went on to Betsy. *Betsy,* says I, *seems of a sweet mild Temper, and if we should give her a Country Squire, and he should happen to be of a rough, passionate Turn, and be angry now and then, it might break her Heart.* "O, none of 'em must be so; for then they would not be good Husbands." *To make sure of this Point, however, for Betsy, shall we give her a Bishop?* "O no, that won't do. They all declare against the Church, and against the Army; not one of them will marry either a Clergyman or an Officer; that they are resolv'd upon." *What can be their reason for that?* "Why you know, that when a Clergyman or an Officer dies, the Income goes with 'em; and then what is there to maintain the Family? There's the Point." *Then suppose we give her a good, honest, sensible City Merchant, who will love her dearly and is very rich?* "I don't know but that may do." We proceeded to Emily, her dear Emily, I was afraid we should hardly find any thing good enough for Emily; but at last, after first settling that, if she did marry, Kitty was to live a good deal with her; we agreed that as Emily was very handsome we might expect an Earl for her: So having fix'd her, as I thought, a Countess, we went on to Anna-Maria. "She," says Kitty, "should have a rich Man that has a large Family and a great many things to take care of; for she is very good at managing, helps my Mama very much, can look over Bills, and order all sorts of Family Business." *Very well; and as there is a Grace and Dignity in her Manner that would become the Station, what do you think of giving her a Duke?* "O no! I'll have the Duke for Emily. You may give the Earl to Anna-Maria if you please: But Emily shall have the Duke." I contested this Matter some time; but at length was forc'd to give up the point, leave Emily in Possession of the Duke, and content myself with the Earl for Anna Maria.

And now what shall we do for Kitty? We have forgot her, all this Time. Well, and what will you do for her? I suppose that tho' the rest have resolv'd against the Army, she may not yet have made so rash a Resolution. "Yes, but she has: Unless, now, an old one, an old General that has done fighting, and is rich, such a one as General Rufane; I like him a good deal; You must know I like an old Man, indeed I do: And some how or other all the old Men take to me, all that come to our House like me better than my other Sisters: I go to 'em and ask 'em how they do, and they like it mightily; and the Maids take notice of it, and say when they see an old Man come, there's a Friend of yours, Miss Kitty." *But then as you like an old General, hadn't you better take him while he's a young Officer, and let him grow old upon your Hands, because then, you'll like him better and bet-*

ter every Year as he grows older and older. "No, that won't do. He must be an old Man of 70 or 80, and take me when I am about 30: And then you know I may be a rich young Widow."

We din'd at Staines, she was Mrs. Shipley, cut up the Chicken pretty handily (with a little Direction) and help'd me in a very womanly Manner. "Now," says she, when I commended her, "my Father never likes to see me or Georgiana carve, because we do it, he says, so badly: But how should we learn if we never try?" We drank good Papa and Mama's Health, and the Health's of the Dutchess, the Countess, the Merchant's Lady, the Country Gentlewoman, and our Welsh Brother. This brought their Affairs again under Consideration. "I doubt," says she, "we have not done right for Betsey. I don't think a Merchant will do for her. She is much inclin'd to be a fine Gentlewoman; and is indeed already more of the fine Gentlewoman, I think, than any of my other Sisters; and therefore she shall be a Vice Countess."

Thus we chatted on, and she was very entertaining quite to Town.

I have now made my Letter as much too long as it was at first too short. The Bishop would think it too trifling, therefore don't show it him. I am afraid too that you will think it so, and have a good mind not to send it. Only it tells you Kitty is well at School, and for that I let it go. My Love to the whole amiable Family, best Respects to the Bishop, and 1000

Thanks for all your Kindnesses, and for the happy Days I enjoy'd at Twyford. With the greatest Esteem and Respect, I am, Madam,

Your most obedient humble Servant

—Writings

৵

Letter to Georgiana ("Kitty") Shipley, "Alas! poor Mungo!" (September 26, 1772)

[Franklin writes now to Kitty Shipley, the young daughter of Franklin's friend, the Bishop of St. Asaph, Jonathan Shipley.]

Dear Miss,

I lament with you most sincerely the unfortunate End of poor *Mungo*: Few Squirrels were better accomplish'd; for he had had a good Education, had travell'd far, and seen much of the World. As he had the Honour of being for his Virtues your Favourite, he should not go like common Skuggs without an Elegy or an Epitaph. Let us give him one in the monumental Stile and Measure, which being neither Prose nor Verse, is perhaps the properest for Grief; since to use common Language would look as if we were not affected, and to make Rhimes would seem Trifling in Sorrow.

Alas! poor *Mungo!* Happy wert thou, hadst thou known Thy own Felicity! Remote from the fierce Bald-Eagle, Tyrant of thy native Woods, Thou hadst nought to fear from his piercing Talons; Nor from the murdering Gun Of the thoughtless Sportsman. Safe in thy wired Castle, Grimalkin never could annoy thee. Daily wert thou fed with the choicest Viands By the fair Hand Of an indulgent Mistress. But, discontented, thou wouldst have more Freedom. Too soon, alas! didst thou obtain it, And, wandering, Fell by the merciless Fangs, Of wanton, cruel Ranger. Learn hence, ye who blindly wish more Liberty, Whether Subjects, Sons, Squirrels or Daughters, That apparent *Restraint* may be real *Protection*, Yielding Peace, Plenty, and Security.

You see how much more decent and proper this broken Stile, interrupted as it were with Sighs, is for the Occasion, than if one were to say, by way of Epitaph,

> Here Skugg
> Lies snug
> As a Bug
> In a Rug.

And yet perhaps there are People in the World of so little Feeling as to think, that would be a good-enough Epitaph for our poor Mungo!

If you wish it, I shall procure another to succeed him. But perhaps you will now chuse some other Amusement. Remember me respectfully to all the good Family; and believe me ever,

Your affectionate Friend

—Writings

❧

Rules for Reducing a Great Empire to a Small One, Presented to a Late Minister, When He Entered upon His Administration (September 11, 1773)

An ancient Sage valued himself upon this, that tho' he could not fiddle, he knew how to make a great City of a little one. The Science that I, a modern Simpleton, am about to communicate is the very reverse.

I address myself to all Ministers who have the Management of extensive Dominions, which from their very Greatness are become troublesome to govern, because the Multiplicity of their Affairs leaves no Time for fiddling.

I. In the first Place, Gentlemen, you are to consider, that a great Empire, like a great Cake, is most easily diminished at the Edges. Turn your Attention therefore first to your *remotest* Provinces; that as you get rid of them, the next may follow in Order.

II. That the Possibility of this Separation may always exist, take special Care the Provinces are *never incorporated with the Mother Country,* that they do not enjoy the same common Rights, the same Privileges in Commerce, and that they are governed by severer Laws, all of your enacting, without allowing them any Share in the Choice of the Legislators. By carefully making and preserving such Distinctions, you will (to keep to my Simile of the Cake) act like a wise Gingerbread Baker, who, to facilitate a Division, cuts his Dough half through in those Places, where, when bak'd, he would have it broken to Pieces.

III. These remote Provinces have perhaps been acquired, purchas'd, or conquer'd, at the sole Expence of the Settlers or their Ancestors, without the Aid of the Mother Country. If this should happen to increase her Strength by their growing Numbers ready to join in her Wars, her Commerce by their growing Demand for her Manufactures, or her Naval Power by greater Employment for her Ships and Seamen, they may probably suppose some Merit in this, and that it entitles them to some Favour; you are therefore to *forget it all, or resent it* as if they had done you Injury. If they happen to be zealous Whigs, Friends of Liberty, nurtur'd in Revolution Principles, remember all that to their Prejudice, and contrive to punish it: For such Principles, after a Revolution is thoroughly established, are of no more Use, they are even odious and abominable.

IV. However peaceably your Colonies have submitted to your Government, shewn their Affection to your Interest, and patiently borne their Grievances, you are to suppose them *always inclined to revolt,* and treat them accordingly. Quarter Troops among them, who by their Insolence may provoke the rising of Mobs, and by their Bullets and Bayonets suppress them. By this Means, like the Husband who uses his Wife ill from Suspicion, you may in Time convert your Suspicions into Realities.

V. Remote Provinces must have Governors, and Judges, to represent the Royal Person, and execute every where the delegated Parts of his Office and Authority. You Ministers know, that much of the Strength of Government depends on the Opinion of the People; and much of that Opinion on the *Choice of Rulers* placed immediately over them. If you send them wise and good Men for Governors, who study the Interest of the Colonists, and advance their Prosperity, they will think their King wise and good, and that he wishes the Welfare of his Subjects. If you send them learned and upright Men for Judges, they will think him a Lover of Justice. This may attach your Provinces more to his Government. You are therefore to be careful who you recommend for those Offices.—If you can find Prodigals who have ruined their Fortunes, broken Gamesters or Stock-Jobbers, these may do well as Governors; for they will probably be rapacious, and provoke the People by their Extortions. Wrangling

Proctors and petty-fogging Lawyers too are not amiss, for they will be for ever disputing and quarrelling with their little Parliaments. If withal they should be ignorant, wrong-headed and insolent, so much the better. Attorneys Clerks and Newgate Solicitors will do for Chief-Justices, especially if they hold their Places during your Pleasure:—And all will contribute to impress those ideas of your Government that are proper for a People you would wish to renounce it.

VI. To confirm these Impressions, and strike them deeper, whenever the Injured come to the Capital with Complaints of Mal-administration, Oppression, or Injustice, *punish such Suitors* with long Delay, enormous Expence, and a final Judgment in Favour of the Oppressor. This will have an admirable Effect every Way. The Trouble of future Complaints will be prevented, and Governors and Judges will be encouraged to farther Acts of Oppression and Injustice; and thence the People may become more disaffected, and at length desperate.

VII. When such Governors have crammed their Coffers, and made themselves so odious to the People that they can no longer remain among them with Safety to their Persons, *recall and reward* them with Pensions. You may make them Baronets too, if that respectable Order should not think fit to resent it. All will contribute to encourage new Governors in the same Practices, and make the supreme Government detestable.

VIII. If when you are engaged in War, your Colonies should vie in liberal Aids of Men and Money against the common Enemy, upon your simple Requisition, and give far beyond their Abilities, reflect, that a Penny taken from them by your Power is more honourable to you than a Pound presented by their Benevolence. *Despise therefore their voluntary Grants,* and resolve to harrass them with *novel Taxes.* They will probably complain to your Parliaments that they are taxed by a Body in which they have no Representative, and that this is contrary to common Right. They will petition for Redress. Let the Parliaments flout their Claims, reject their Petitions, refuse even to suffer the reading of them, and treat the Petitioners with the utmost Contempt. Nothing can have a better Effect, in producing the Alienation proposed; for though many can forgive Injuries, none ever forgave Contempt.

IX. In laying these Taxes, *never regard the heavy Burthens* those remote People already undergo, in defending their own Frontiers, supporting their own provincial Governments, making new Roads, building Bridges, Churches and other public Edifices, which in old Countries have been done to your Hands by your Ancestors, but which occasion constant Calls and Demands on the Purses of a new People. Forget the Restraints you lay on their Trade for your own Benefit, and the Advantage a Monopoly of this Trade gives your exacting Merchants. Think nothing of the

Wealth those Merchants and your Manufacturers acquire by the Colony Commerce; their encreased Ability thereby to pay Taxes at home; their accumulating, in the Price of their Commodities, most of those Taxes, and so levying them from their consuming Customers: All this, and the Employment and Support of Thousands of your Poor by the Colonists, you are intirely to forget. But remember to make your arbitrary Tax more grievous to your Provinces, by public Declarations importing that your Power of taxing them has no Limits, so that when you take from them without their Consent a Shilling in the Pound, you have a clear Right to the other nineteen. This will probably weaken every Idea of Security in their Property, and convince them that under such a Government they have nothing they can call their own; which can scarce fail of producing the happiest Consequences!

X. Possibly indeed some of them might still comfort themselves, and say, "Though we have no Property, we have yet something left that is valuable; we have constitutional *Liberty both of Person and of Conscience.* This King, these Lords, and these Commons, who it seems are too remote from us to know us and feel for us, cannot take from us our Habeas Corpus Right, or our Right of Trial by a Jury of our Neighbours: They cannot deprive us of the Exercise of our Religion, alter our ecclesiastical Constitutions, and compel us to be Papists if they please, or Mahometans." To annihilate this Comfort, begin by Laws to perplex their Commerce with infinite Regulations impossible to be remembered and observed; ordain Seizures of their Property for every Failure; take away the Trial of such Property by Jury, and give it to arbitrary Judges of your own appointing, and of the lowest Characters in the Country, whose Salaries and Emoluments are to arise out of the Duties or Condemnations, and whose Appointments are during Pleasure. Then let there be a formal Declaration of both Houses, that Opposition to your Edicts is Treason, and that Persons suspected of Treason in the Provinces may, according to some obsolete Law, be seized and sent to the Metropolis of the Empire for Trial; and pass an Act that those there charged with certain other Offences shall be sent away in Chains from their Friends and Country to be tried in the same Manner for Felony. Then erect a new Court of Inquisition among them, accompanied by an armed Force, with Instructions to transport all such suspected Persons, to be ruined by the Expence if they bring over Evidences to prove their Innocence, or be found guilty and hanged if they can't afford it. And lest the People should think you cannot possibly go any farther, pass another solemn declaratory Act, that "King, Lords, and Commons had, hath, and of Right ought to have, full Power and Authority to make Statutes of sufficient Force and Validity to bind the unrepresented Provinces *in all cases whatsoever.*" This will include spiritual with temporal; and taken together, must operate wonderfully to your Purpose, by convincing them, that they are at present under a Power something like that spoken of in the Scriptures, which can not only kill their Bodies, but damn their Souls to all Eternity, by compelling them, if it pleases, to worship the Devil.

XI. To make your Taxes more odious, and more likely to procure Resistance, send from the Capital a *Board of Officers* to superintend the Collection, *composed of the most indiscreet,* ill-bred and insolent you can find. Let these have large Salaries out of the extorted Revenue, and live in open grating Luxury upon the Sweat and Blood of the Industrious, whom they are to worry continually with groundless and expensive Prosecutions before the above-mentioned arbitrary Revenue-Judges, all at the Cost of the Party prosecuted tho' acquitted, because the King is to pay no Costs.—Let these Men by your Order be exempted from all the common Taxes and Burthens of the Province, though they and their Property are protected by its Laws. If any Revenue Officers are suspected of the least Tenderness for the People, discard them. If others are justly complained of, protect and reward them. If any of the Under-officers behave so as to provoke the People to drub them, promote those to better Offices: This will encourage others to procure for themselves such profitable Drubbings, by multiplying and enlarging such Provocations, and all with work towards the End you aim at.

XII. Another Way to make your Tax odious, is to *misapply the Produce of it.* If it was originally appropriated for the Defence of the Provinces and the better Support of Government, and the Administration of Justice where it may be necessary, then apply none of it to that Defence, but bestow it where it is not necessary, in augmented Salaries or Pensions to every Governor who has distinguished himself by his Enmity to the People, and by calumniating them to their Sovereign. This will make them pay it more unwillingly, and be more apt to quarrel with those that collect it, and those that imposed it, who will quarrel again with them, and all shall contribute to your main Purpose of making them weary of your Government.

XIII. If the People of any Province have been accustomed to *support their own Governors and Judges* to Satisfaction, you are to apprehend that such Governors and Judges may be thereby influenced to treat the People kindly, and to do them Justice. This is another Reason for applying Part of that Revenue in larger Salaries to such Governors and Judges, given, as their Commissions are, during your Pleasure only, forbidding them to take any Salaries from their Provinces; that thus the People may no longer hope any Kindness from their Governors, or (in Crown Cases) any Justice from their Judges. And as the Money thus mis-applied in one Province is extorted from all, probably all will resent the Mis-application.

XIV. If the Parliaments of your Provinces should dare to claim Rights or complain of your Administration, order them to be harass'd with *repeated Dissolutions.* If the same Men are continually return'd by new Elections, adjourn their Meetings to some Country Village where they cannot be accommodated, and there keep them during Pleasure; for this, you know, is your PREROGATIVE; and an excellent one it is, as you may manage it, to promote Discontents among the People, diminish their Respect, and increase their Dis-affection.

XV. Convert the brave honest Officers of your *Navy* into pimping Tide-waiters and Colony Officers of the *Customs.* Let those who in Time of War fought gallantly in Defence of the Commerce of their Countrymen, in Peace be taught to prey upon it. Let them learn to be corrupted by great and real Smugglers, but (to shew their Diligence) scour with armed Boats every Bay, Harbour, River, Creek, Cove or Nook throughout the Coast of your Colonies, stop and detain every Coaster, every Wood-boat, every Fisherman, tumble their Cargoes, and even their Ballast, inside out and upside down; and if a Penn'orth of Pins is found un-entered, let the Whole be seized and confiscated. Thus shall the Trade of your Colonists suffer more from their Friends in Time of Peace, than it did from their Enemies in War. Then let these Boats Crews land upon every Farm in their Way, rob the Orchards, steal the Pigs and Poultry, and insult the Inhabitants. If the injured and exasperated Farmers, unable to procure other Justice, should attack the Agressors, drub them and burn their Boats, you are to call this *High Treason and Rebellion,* order Fleets and Armies into their Country, and threaten to carry all the Offenders three thousand Miles to be hang'd, drawn and quartered. O! this will work admirably!

XVI. If you are told of *Discontents* in your Colonies, never believe that they are general, or that you have given Occasion for them; therefore do not think of applying any Remedy, or of changing any offensive Measure. Redress no Grievance, lest they should be encouraged to demand the Redress of some other Grievance. Grant no Request that is just and reasonable, lest they should make another that is unreasonable. Take all your Informations of the State of the Colonies from your Governors and Officers in Enmity with them. Encourage and reward these Leasing-makers; secrete their lying Accusations lest they should be confuted; but act upon them as the clearest Evidence, and believe nothing you hear from the Friends of the People. Suppose all their Complaints to be invented and promoted by a few factious Demagogues, whom if you could catch and hang, all would be quiet. Catch and hang a few of them accordingly; and the Blood of the Martyrs shall work Miracles in favour of your Purpose.

XVII. If you see *rival Nations* rejoicing at the Prospect of your Disunion with your Provinces, and endeavouring to promote it: If they translate,

publish and applaud all the Complaints of your discontented Colonists, at the same Time privately stimulating you to severer Measures; let not that alarm or offend you. Why should it? since you all mean the same Thing.

XVIII. If any Colony should *at their own Charge erect a Fortress* to secure their Port against the Fleets of a foreign Enemy, get your Governor to betray that Fortress into your Hands. Never think of paying what it cost the Country, for that would look, at least, like some Regard for Justice; but turn it into a Citadel to awe the Inhabitants and curb their Commerce. If they should have lodged in such Fortress the very Arms they bought and used to aid you in your Conquests, seize them all, 'twill provoke like Ingratitude added to Robbery. One admirable Effect of these Operations will be, to discourage every other Colony from erecting such Defences, and so their and your Enemies may more easily invade them, to the great Disgrace of your Government, and of course the Furtherance of your Project.

XIX. Send Armies into their Country under Pretence of protecting the Inhabitants; but instead of garrisoning the Forts on their Frontiers with those Troops, to prevent Incursions, demolish those Forts, and order the Troops into the Heart of the Country, that the Savages may be encouraged to attack the Frontiers, and that the Troops may be protected by the Inhabitants: This will seem to proceed from your *Ill will or your Ignorance,* and contribute farther to produce and strengthen an Opinion among them, that you are no longer fit to govern them.

XX. Lastly, Invest the *General of your Army in the Provinces* with great and unconstitutional Powers, and free him from the Controul of even your own Civil Governors. Let him have Troops enow under his Command, with all the Fortresses in his Possession; and who knows but (like some provincial Generals in the Roman Empire, and encouraged by the universal Discontent you have produced) he may take it into his Head to set up for himself. If he should, and you have carefully practised these few excellent Rules of mine, take my Word for it, all the Provinces will immediately join him, and you will that Day (if you have not done it sooner) get rid of the Trouble of governing them, and all the Plagues attending their Commerce and Connection from thenceforth and for ever.

—*The Public Advertise*

Conversation of a Company of Ephemerae;
With the Soliloquy of One Advanced in Age (c. 1778)

To Madame Brilliant—

You may remember, my dear friend, that when we lately spent that happy day, in the delightful garden and sweet society of the *Moulin Joly*, I stopt a little in one of our walks, and staid some time behind the company. We had been shown numberless skeletons of a kind of little fly, called an ephemera, whose successive generations, we were told, were bred and expired within the day. I happened to see a living company of them on a leaf, who appeared to be engaged in conversation. You know I understand all the inferior animal tongues; my too great application to the study of them is the best excuse I can give for the little progress I have made in your charming language. I listened through curiosity to the discourse of these little creatures, but as they, in their national vivacity, spoke three or four together, I could make but little of their conversation. I found, however, by some broken expressions that I heard now and then, they were disputing warmly on the merit of two foreign musicians, one a cousin, the other a *muscheto*; in which dispute they spent their time, seeming as regardless of the shortness of their life as if they had been sure of living a month. Happy people, thought I, you live certainly under a wise, just, and mild government, since you have no public grievances to complain of, nor any other subject of contention but the perfections or imperfections of foreign music. I turned my head from them to an old grey-headed one, who was single on another leaf, and talking to himself. Being amused with his soliloquy, I put it down in writing, in hopes it will likewise amuse her to whom I am so much indebted for the most pleasing of all amusements—her delicious company and heavenly harmony.

"It was," says he, "the opinion of learned philosophers of our race, who lived and flourished long before my time, that this vast world, the *Moulin Joly*, could not itself subsist more than eighteen hours: and I think there was some foundation for that opinion; since, by the apparent motion of the great luminary that gives light to all nature, and which in my time has evidently declined considerably towards the ocean at the end of the earth, it must then finish its course, be extinguished in the waters that surround us, and leave the world in cold and darkness, necessarily producing universal death and destruction. I have lived seven of those hours: a great age, being no less than 420 minutes of time! How very few of us continue so long! I have seen generations born, flourish, and expire. My present friends are the children and grandchildren of the friends of my youth, who are now, alas, no more! and I must soon follow them; for, by the common course of nature, though still in health, I cannot expect to live above seven or eight minutes longer. What now avails all my toil and labour in amassing honey-dew on this leaf, which I cannot live to enjoy! what the political struggles I have been engaged in, for the good of my compatriot inhabitants of this bush, or my philosophical studies, for the benefit of our race in general: for in polities (what can laws do without morals!) our present race of ephemerae will in a course of minutes become corrupt, like those of other and older bushes, and consequently as wretched! And in philosophy how small our progress! Alas! art is long, and life is short! My friends would comfort me with the idea of a name, they say, I shall leave behind me; and they tell me I have lived long enough to nature and to glory. But what will fame be to an ephemera who no longer exists! and what will become of all history in the eighteenth hour, when the world itself, even the whole *Moulin Joly*, shall come to its end, and be buried in a universal ruin!"

To me, after all my eager pursuits, no solid pleasures now remain, but the reflection of a long life spent in meaning well, the sensible conversation of a few good lady ephemerae, and now and then a kind smile and a tune from the ever amiable Brilliant.

B. FRANKLIN

—Writings

Letter to Madame Brillon, "The Whistle" (November 10, 1779)

Passy, France

I received my dear friend's two letters, one for Wednesday and one for Saturday. This is again Wednesday. I do not deserve one for to-day, because I have not answered the former. But, indolent as I am, and averse to writing, the fear of having no more of your pleasing epistles, if I do not contribute to the correspondence, obliges me to take up my pen; and as Mr. B. has kindly sent me word that he sets out to-morrow to see you, instead of spending this Wednesday evening, as I have done its namesakes, in your delightful company, I sit down to spend it in thinking of you, in writing to you, and in reading over and over again your letters.

I am charmed with your description of Paradise, and with your plan of living there; and I approve much of your conclusion, that, in the meantime, we should draw all the good we can from this world. In my opinion we might all draw more good from it than we do, and suffer less evil, if we would take care not to give too much for *whistles*. For to me it seems that most of the unhappy people we meet with are become so by neglect of that caution.

You ask what I mean? You love stories, and will excuse my telling one of myself.

When I was a child of seven years old, my friends, on a holiday, filled my pocket with coppers. I went directly to a shop where they sold toys for children; and being charmed with the sound of a *whistle*, that I met by the way in the hands of another boy, I voluntarily offered and gave all my money for one. I then came home, and went whistling all over the house, much pleased with my *whistle*, but disturbing all the family. My brothers, and sisters, and cousins, understanding the bargain I had made, told me I had given four times as much for it as it was worth; put me in mind what good things I might have bought with the rest of the money; and laughed at me so much for my folly, that I cried with vexation; and the reflection gave me more chagrin than the *whistle* gave me pleasure.

This, however, was afterwards of use to me, the impression continuing on my mind; so that often, when I was tempted to buy some unnecessary thing, I said to myself, *Don't give too much for the whistle*; and so I saved my money.

As I grew up, came into the world, and observed the actions of men, I thought I met with many, very many, *who gave too much for the whistle*.

When I saw one too ambitious of court favor, sacrificing his time in attendance on levees, his repose, his liberty, his virtue, and perhaps his friends, to attain it, I have said to myself, this man gives too much for his whistle.

When I saw another fond of popularity, constantly employing himself in political bustles, neglecting his own affairs, and ruining them by that neglect, *He pays, indeed,* says I, *too much for his whistle.*

If I knew a miser, who gave up every kind of comfortable living, all the pleasure of doing good to others, all the esteem of his fellow-citizens, and the joys of benevolent friendship, for the sake of accumulating wealth, *Poor man,* says I, *you pay too much for your whistle.*

When I met with a man of pleasure, sacrificing every laudable improvement of the mind, or of his fortune, to mere corporeal sensations, and ruining his health in their pursuit, *Mistaken man,* says I, *you are providing pain for yourself, instead of pleasure; you give too much for your whistle.*

If I see one fond of appearance, or fine clothes, fine houses, fine furniture, fine equipages, all above his fortune, for which he contracts debts, and ends his career in a prison, *Alas,* says I, *he has paid dear, very dear, for his whistle.*

When I see a beautiful sweet-tempered girl married to an ill-natured brute of a husband, *What a pity,* says I, *that she should pay so much for a whistle!*

In short, I conceive that great part of the miseries of mankind are brought upon them by the false estimates they have made of the value of things, and by their giving too much for their *whistles.*

Yet I ought to have charity for these unhappy people, when I consider that, with all this wisdom of which I am boasting, there are certain things in the world so tempting, for example, the apples of King John, which happily are not to be bought; for if they were put to sale by auction, I might very easily be led to ruin myself in the purchase, and find that I had once more given too much for the *whistle.*

Adieu, my dear friend, and believe me ever yours very sincerely and with unalterable affection,

B. FRANKLIN

—Writings

✌

Dialogue between Franklin and the Gout (October 22, 1780)

Midnight.

FRANKLIN: Eh! Oh! Eh! What have I done to merit these cruel sufferings?

GOUT: Many things; you have ate and drank too freely, and too much indulged those legs of yours in their indolence.

FRANKLIN: Who is it that accuses me?

GOUT: It is I, even I, the Gout.

FRANKLIN: What! my enemy in person?

GOUT: No, not your enemy.

FRANKLIN: I repeat it; my enemy; for you would not only torment my body to death, but ruin my good name; you reproach me as a glutton and a tippler; now all the world, that knows me, will allow that I am neither the one nor the other.

GOUT: The world may think as it pleases; it is always very complaisant to itself, and sometimes to its friends; but I very well know that the quantity of meat and drink proper for a man, who takes a reasonable degree of exercise, would be too much for another, who never takes any.

FRANKLIN: I take—Eh! Oh!—as much exercise—Eh!—as I can, Madam Gout. You know my sedentary state, and on that account, it would seem, Madam Gout, as if you might spare me a little, seeing it is not altogether my own fault.

GOUT: Not a jot; your rhetoric and your politeness are thrown away; your apology avails nothing. If your situation in life is a sedentary one, your amusements, your recreations, at least, should be active. You ought to walk or ride; or, if the weather prevents that play at billiards. But let us examine your course of life. While the mornings are long, and you have leisure to go abroad, what do you do? Why, instead of gaining an appetite for breakfast, by salutary exercise, you amuse yourself, with books, pamphlets, or newspapers, which commonly are not worth the reading. Yet you eat an inordinate breakfast, four dishes of tea, with cream, and one or two buttered toasts, with slices of hung beef, which I fancy are not things the most easily digested. Immediately afterward you sit down to write at your desk, or converse with persons who apply to you on business. Thus the time passes till one, without any kind of bodily exercise. But all this I could pardon, in regard, as you say, to your sedentary condition. But what is your practice after dinner? Walking in the beautiful gardens of those friends, with whom you have dined, would be the choice of men of sense; yours is to be fixed down to chess, where you are found engaged for two or three hours! This is your perpetual recreation, which is the least eligible of any for a sedentary man, because, instead of accelerating the motion of the fluids, the rigid attention it requires helps to retard the circulation and obstruct internal secretions. Wrapt in the speculations of this wretched game, you destroy your constitution. What can be expected from such a course of living, but a body replete with stagnant humours, ready to fall a prey to all kinds of dangerous maladies, if I, the Gout, did not occasionally bring you relief by agitating those humours, and so purifying or dissipating them? If it was in some nook or alley in Paris, deprived of walks, that you played awhile at chess after dinner, this might be excusable; but the same taste prevails with you in Passy,

Auteuil, Montmartre, or Savoy, places where there are the finest gardens and walks, a pure air, beautiful women, and most agreeable and instructive conversation; all which you might enjoy by frequenting the walks. But these are rejected for this abominable game of chess. Fie, then, Mr. Franklin! But amidst my instructions, I had almost forgot to administer my wholesome corrections; so take that twinge,—and that.

FRANKLIN: Oh! Eh! Oh! Ohhh! As much instruction as you please, Madam Gout, and as many reproaches; but pray, Madam, a truce with your corrections!

GOUT: No, Sir, no,—I will not abate a particle of what is so much for your good,—therefore—

FRANKLIN: Oh! Ehhh!—It is not fair to say I take no exercise, when I do very often, going out to dine and returning in my carriage.

GOUT: That, of all imaginable exercises, is the most slight and insignificant, if you allude to the motion of a carriage suspended on springs. By observing the degree of heat obtained by different kinds of motion, we may form an estimate of the quantity of exercise given by each. Thus, for example, if you turn out to walk in winter with cold feet, in an hour's time you will be in a glow all over; ride on horseback, the same effect will scarcely be perceived by four hours' round trotting; but if you loll in a carriage, such as you have mentioned, you may travel all day, and gladly enter the last inn to warm your feet by a fire. Flatter yourself then no longer, that half an hour's airing in your carriage deserves the name of exercise. Providence has appointed few to roll in carriages, while he has given to all a pair of legs, which are machines infinitely more commodious and serviceable. Be grateful, then, and make a proper use of yours. Would you know how they forward the circulation of your fluids, in the very action of transporting you from place to place; observe when you walk, that all your weight is alternately thrown from one leg to the other; this occasions a great pressure on the vessels of the foot, and repels their contents; when relieved, by the weight being thrown on the other foot, the vessels of the first are allowed to replenish, and, by a return of this weight, this repulsion again succeeds; thus accelerating the circulation of the blood. The heat produced in any given time, depends on the degree of this acceleration; the fluids are shaken, the humours attenuated, the secretions facilitated, and all goes well; the cheeks are ruddy, and health is established. Behold your fair friend at Auteuil, a lady who received from bounteous nature more really useful science, than half a dozen such pretenders to philosophy as you have been able to extract from all your books. When she honours you with a visit, it is on foot. She walks all hours of the day, and leaves indolence, and its concomitant maladies, to be endured by her horses. In this see at once the preservative of her health and personal charms. But when you go to Auteuil, you must have your carriage, though it is no further from Passy to Auteuil than from Auteuil to Passy.

FRANKLIN: Your reasonings grow very tiresome.

GOUT: I stand corrected. I will be silent and continue my office; take that, and that.

FRANKLIN: Oh! Ohh! Talk on, I pray you!

GOUT: No, no; I have a good number of twinges for you to-night, and you may be sure of some more to-morrow.

FRANKLIN: What, with such a fever! I shall go distracted. Oh! Eh! Can no one bear it for me?

GOUT: Ask that of your horses; they have served you faithfully.

FRANKLIN: How can you so cruelly sport with my torments?

GOUT: Sport! I am very serious. I have here a list of offences against your own health distinctly written, and can justify every stroke inflicted on you.

FRANKLIN: Read it then.

GOUT: It is too long a detail; but I will briefly mention some particulars.

FRANKLIN: Proceed. I am all attention.

GOUT: Do you remember how often you have promised yourself, the following morning, a walk in the grove of Boulogne, in the garden de la Muette, or in your own garden, and have violated your promise, alleging, at one time, it was too cold, at another too warm, too windy, too moist, or what else you pleased; when in truth it was too nothing, but your insuperable love of ease?

FRANKLIN: That I confess may have happened occasionally, probably ten times in a year.

GOUT: Your confession is very far short of the truth; the gross amount is one hundred and ninety-nine times.

FRANKLIN: Is it possible?

GOUT: So possible, that it is fact; you may rely on the accuracy of my statement. You know M. Brillon's gardens, and what fine walks they contain; you know the handsome flight of an hundred steps, which lead from the terrace above to the lawn below. You have been in the practice of visiting this amiable family twice a week, after dinner, and it is a maxim of your own, that "a man may take as much exercise in walking a mile, up and down stairs, as in ten on level ground." What an opportunity was here for you to have had exercise in both these ways! Did you embrace it, and how often?

FRANKLIN: I cannot immediately answer that question.

GOUT: I will do it for you; not once.

FRANKLIN: Not once?

GOUT: Even so. During the summer you went there at six o'clock. You found the charming lady, with her lovely children and friends, eager to walk with you, and entertain you with their agreeable conversation; and what has been your choice? Why to sit on the terrace, satisfying yourself with the fine prospect, and passing your eye over the beauties of the garden below, without taking one step to descend and walk about in them. On the contrary, you call for tea and the chess-board; and lo! you are occupied in your seat till nine o'clock, and that besides two hours' play after dinner; and then, instead of walking home, which would have bestirred you a little, you step into your carriage. How absurd to suppose that all this carelessness can be reconcilable with health, without my interposition!

FRANKLIN: I am convinced now of the justness of poor Richard's remark, that "Our debts and our sins are always greater than we think for."

GOUT: So it is. You philosophers are sages in your maxims, and fools in your conduct.

FRANKLIN: But do you charge among my crimes, that I return in a carriage from Mr. Brillon's?

GOUT: Certainly; for, having been seated all the while, you cannot object the fatigue of the day, and cannot want therefore the relief of a carriage.

FRANKLIN: What then would you have me do with my carriage?

GOUT: Burn it if you choose; you would at least get heat out of it once in this way; or, if you dislike that proposal, here's another for you; observe the poor peasants, who work in the vineyards and grounds about the villages of Passy, Auteuil, Chaillot, &c.; you may find every day, among these deserving creatures, four or five old men and women, bent and perhaps crippled by weight of years, and too long and too great labour. After a most fatiguing day, these people have to trudge a mile or two to their smoky huts. Order your coachman to set them down. This is an act that will be good for your soul; and, at the same time, after your visit to the Brillons, if you return on foot, that will be good for your body.

FRANKLIN: Ah! how tiresome you are!

GOUT: Well, then, to my office; it should not be forgotten that I am your physician. There.

FRANKLIN: Ohhh! what a devil of a physician!

GOUT: How ungrateful you are to say so! Is it not I who, in the character of your physician, have saved you from the palsy, dropsy, and apoplexy? one or other of which would have done for you long ago, but for me.

FRANKLIN: I submit, and thank you for the past, but entreat the discontinuance of your visits for the future; for, in my mind, one had better die than be cured so dolefully. Permit me just to hint, that I have also not been unfriendly to you. I never feed physician or quack of any kind, to enter the list against you; if then you do not leave me to my repose, it may be said you are ungrateful too.

GOUT: I can scarcely acknowledge that as any objection. As to quacks, I despise them; they may kill you indeed, but cannot injure me. And, as to regular physicians, they are at last convinced that the gout, in such a subject as you are, is no disease, but a remedy; and wherefore cure a remedy?—but to our business,—there.

FRANKLIN: Oh! oh!—for Heaven's sake leave me! and I promise faithfully never more to play at chess, but to take exercise daily, and live temperately.

GOUT: I know you too well. You promise fair; but, after a few months of good health, you will return to your old habits; your fine promises will be forgotten like the forms of last year's clouds. Let us then finish the account, and I will go. But I leave you with an assurance of visiting you again at a proper time and place; for my object is your good, and you are sensible now that I am your real friend.

—Writings

The Handsome and Deformed Leg (1780?)

There are two Sorts of People in the World, who with equal Degrees of Health, & Wealth, and the other Comforts of Life, become, the one happy, and the other miserable. This arises very much from the different Views in which they consider Things, Persons, and Events; and the Effect of those different Views upon their own Minds.

In whatever Situation Men can be plac'd, they may find Convenienc-es & Inconveniences: In whatever Company; they may find Persons & Conversation more or less pleasing. At whatever Table, they may meet with Meats & Drinks of better and worse Taste, Dishes better & worse dress'd: In whatever Climate they will find good and bad Weather: Under whatever Government, they may find good & bad Laws, and good & bad Administration of those Laws. In every Poem or Work of Genius they may see Faults and Beauties. In almost every Face & every Person, they may discover fine Features & Defects, good and bad Qualities.

Under these Circumstances, the two Sorts of People above mention'd fix their Attention, those who are to be happy, on the Conveniences of Things, the pleasant Parts of Conversation, the well-dress'd Dishes, the Goodness of the Wines, the fine Weather; &c, and enjoy all with Chear-fulness. Those who are to be unhappy, think & speak only of the contraries. Hence they are continually discontented themselves, and by their Remarks sour the Pleasures of Society, offend personally many People, and make themselves everywhere disagreable. If this Turn of Mind was founded in Nature, such unhappy Persons would be the more to be pitied. But as the Disposition to criticise, & be disgusted, is perhaps taken up originally by Imitation, and is unawares grown into a Habit, which tho' at present strong may nevertheless be cured when those who have it are convinc'd of its bad Effects on their Felicity; I hope this little Admonition may be of Service to them, and put them on changing a Habit, which tho' in the Exercise it is chiefly an Act of Imagination yet has serious Consequences in Life, as it brings on real Griefs and Misfortunes. For as many are offended by, & nobody well loves this Sort of People, no one shows them more than the most common civility and respect, and scarcely that; and this frequently puts them out of humour, and draws them into disputes and contentions. If they aim at obtaining some advantage in rank or fortune, nobody wishes them success, or will stir a step, or speak a word, to favour their pretensions. If they incur public censure or disgrace, no one will defend or excuse, and many join to aggravate their misconduct, and render them completely odious. If these people will not change this bad habit, and condescend to be pleased with what is pleasing, without fretting themselves and others about the contraries, it is good for others to avoid an acquaintance with them; which is always disagreeable, and sometimes very inconvenient, especially when one finds one's self entangled in their quarrels.

An old philosophical friend of mine was grown, from experience, very cautious in this particular, and carefully avoided any intimacy with such people. He had, like other philosophers, a thermometer to show him the heat of the weather, and a barometer to mark when it was likely to prove good or bad; but, there being no instrument in vented to discover, at first sight, this unpleasing disposition in a person, he for that purpose made use of his legs; one of which was remarkably handsome, the other, by some accident, crooked and deformed. If a Stranger, at the first interview, regarded his ugly Leg more than his handsome one, he doubted him. If he spoke of it, & took no notice of the handsome Leg, that was sufficient to determine my Philosopher to have no further Acquaintance with him. Every body has not this two-legged Instrument, but every one with a little Attention, may observe Signs of that carping, fault-finding Disposition, & take the same Resolution of avoiding the Acquaintance of those infected with it. I therefore advise those critical, querulous, discontented, unhappy People, that if they wish to be respected and belov'd by others, & happy in themselves they should *leave off looking at the ugly Leg.*

—Writings

Letter to Richard Price, "Advantages of the Press" (June 13, 1782)

The ancient Roman and Greek orators could only speak to the number of citizens capable of being assembled within the reach of their voice; their writings had little effect, because the bulk of the people could not read. Now by the press we can speak to nations; and good books, and well-written pamphlets, have great and general influence. The facility with which the same truths may be repeatedly enforced by placing them in different lights, in newspapers which are everywhere read, gives a great chance of establishing them. And we now find that it is not only right to strike while the iron is hot, but that it is very practicable to heat it by continual striking.

—Writings

❧

Remarks Concerning the Savages of North America (1784)

Savages we call them, because their manners differ from ours, which we think the perfection of civility; they think the same of theirs.

Perhaps, if we could examine the manners of different nations with impartiality, we should find no people so rude, as to be without any rules of politeness; nor any so polite, as not to have some remains of rudeness.

The Indian men, when young, are hunters and warriors; when old, counsellors; for all their government is by the counsel or advice of the sages; there is no force, there are no prisons, no officers to compel obedience, or inflict punishment. Hence they generally study oratory, the best speaker having the most influence. The Indian women till the ground, dress the food, nurse and bring up the children, and preserve and hand down to posterity the memory of public transactions. These employments of men and women are accounted natural and honorable. Having few artificial wants, they have abundance of leisure for improvement by conversation. Our laborious manner of life, compared with theirs, they esteem slavish and base; and the learning, on which we value ourselves, they regard as frivolous and useless. ....

Having frequent occasions to hold public councils, they have acquired great order and decency in conducting them. The old men sit in the foremost ranks, the warriors in the next, and the women and children in the hindmost. The business of the women is to take exact notice of what passes, imprint it in their memories (for they have no writing), and communicate it to their children. They are the records of the council, and they preserve the tradition of the stipulations in treaties a hundred years back; which, when we compare with our writings, we always find exact. He that would speak, rises. The rest observe a profound silence. When he has finished and sits down, they leave him five or six minutes to recollect, that, if he has omitted any thing he intended to say, or has any thing to add, he may rise again and deliver it. To interrupt another, even in common conversation, is reckoned highly indecent. How different this is from the conduct of a polite British House of Commons, where scarce a day passes without some confusion, that makes the speaker hoarse in calling to order; and how different from the mode of conversation in many polite companies of Europe, where, if you do not deliver your sentence with great rapidity, you are cut off in the middle of it by the impatient loquacity of those you converse with, and never suffered to finish it!

The politeness of these savages in conversation is indeed carried to excess, since it does not permit them to contradict or deny the truth of what is asserted in their presence. By this means they indeed avoid disputes; but then it becomes difficult to know their minds, or what impression you make upon them. The missionaries who have attempted to convert them to Christianity, all complain of this as one of the great difficulties of their mission. The Indians hear with patience the truths of the Gospel explained to them, and give their usual tokens of assent and approbation; you would think they were convinced. No such matter. It is mere civility.

A Swedish minister, having assembled the chiefs of the Susquehanna Indians, made a sermon to them, acquainting them with the principal historical facts on which our religion is founded; such as the fall of our first parents by eating an apple, the coming of Christ to repair the mischief, his miracles and suffering, &c. When he had finished, an Indian orator stood up to thank him. "What you have told us," says he, "is all very good. It is indeed bad to eat apples. It is better to make them all into cider. We are much obliged by your kindness in coming so far, to tell us those things which you have heard from your mothers. In return, I will tell you some of those we have heard from ours. In the beginning, our fathers had only the flesh of animals to subsist on; and, if their hunting was unsuccessful, they were starving. Two of our young hunters, having killed a deer, made a fire in the woods to broil some parts of it. When they were about to satisfy their hunger, they beheld a beautiful young woman descend from the clouds, and seat herself on that hill, which you see yonder among the Blue Mountains. They said to each other, it is a spirit that perhaps has smelt our broiling venison, and wishes to eat of it; let us offer some to her. They presented her with the tongue; she was pleased with the taste of it, and said, 'Your kindness shall be rewarded; come to this place after thirteen moons, and you shall find something that will be of great benefit in nourishing you and your children to the latest generations.' They did so, and, to their surprise, found plants they had never seen before; but which, from that ancient time, have been constantly cultivated among us, to our great advantage. Where her right hand had touched the ground, they found maize; where her left hand had touched it, they found kidney-beans; and where her backside had sat on it, they found tobacco." The good missionary, disgusted with this idle tale, said, "What I delivered to you were sacred truths; but what you tell me is mere fable, fiction, and falsehood."

The Indian, offended, replied, "My brother, it seems your friends have not done you justice in your education; they have not well instructed you in the rules of common civility. You saw that we, who understand and practise those rules, believed all your stories; why do you refuse to believe ours?"

When any of them come into our towns, our people are apt to crowd round them, gaze upon them, and incommode them, where they desire to be private; this they esteem great rudeness, and the effect of the want of instruction in the rules of civility and good manners. "We have," say they, "as much curiosity as you, and when you come into our towns, we wish for opportunities of looking at you; but for this purpose we hide ourselves behind bushes, where you are to pass, and never intrude ourselves into your company."

Their manner of entering one another's village has likewise its rules. It is reckoned uncivil in travelling strangers to enter a village abruptly, without giving notice of their approach. Therefore, as soon as they arrive within hearing, they stop and hollow, remaining there till invited to enter. Two old men usually come out to them, and lead them in. There is in every village a vacant dwelling, called the strangers' house. Here they are placed, while the old men go round from hut to hut, acquainting the inhabitants, that strangers are arrived, who are probably hungry and weary; and every one sends them what he can spare of victuals, and skins to repose on. When the strangers are refreshed, pipes and tobacco are brought; and then, but not before, conversation begins, with inquiries who they are, whither bound, what news, &c.; and it usually ends with offers of service, if the strangers have occasion for guides, or any necessaries for continuing their journey; and nothing is exacted for the entertainment.

The same hospitality, esteemed among them as a principal virtue, is practised by private persons; of which Conrad Weiser, our interpreter, gave me the following instance. He had been naturalized among the Six Nations, and spoke well the Mohock language. In going through the Indian country, to carry a message from our governor to the council at Onondaga, he called at the habitation of Canassetego, an old acquaintance, who embraced him, spread furs for him to sit on, and placed before him some boiled beans and venison, and mixed some rum and water for his drink. When he was well refreshed, and had lit his pipe, Canassetego began to converse with him; asked how he had fared the many years since they had seen each other; whence he then came; what occasioned the journey, &c. Conrad answered all his questions; and when the discourse began to flag, the Indian, to continue it, said, "Conrad, you have lived long among the white people, and know something of their customs; I have been sometimes at Albany, and have observed, that once in seven days they shut up their shops, and assemble all in the great house; tell me what it is for? What do they do there?"

"They meet there," says Conrad, "to hear and learn good things."

"I do not doubt," says the Indian, "that they tell you so; they have told me the same; but I doubt the truth of what they say, and I will tell you my reasons. I went lately to Albany to sell my skins and buy blankets, knives, powder, rum, &c. You know I used generally to deal with Hans Hanson; but I was a little inclined this time to try some other merchants. However, I called first upon Hans, and asked him what he would give for beaver. He said he could not give any more than four shillings a pound; 'but,' says he, 'I cannot talk on business now; this is the day when we meet together to learn good things, and I am going to meeting.' So I thought to myself, 'Since I cannot do any business today, I may as well go to the meeting too,' and I went with him. There stood up a man in black, and began to talk to the people very angrily. I did not understand what he said; but, perceiving that he looked much at me and at Hanson, I imagined he was angry at seeing me there; so I went out, sat down near the house, struck fire, and lit my pipe, waiting till the meeting should break up. I thought too, that the man had mentioned something of beaver, and I suspected it might be the subject of their meeting. So, when they came out, I accosted my merchant. 'Well, Hans,' says I, 'I hope you have agreed to give more than four shillings a pound.' 'No,' says he, 'I cannot give so much; I cannot give more than three shillings and sixpence.' I then spoke to several other dealers, but they all sung the same song,—three and sixpence,—three and sixpence. This made it clear to me, that my suspicion was right; and, that whatever they pretended of meeting to learn good things, the real purpose was to consult how to cheat Indians in the price of beaver. Consider but a little, Conrad, and you must be of my opinion. If they met so often to learn good things, they would certainly have learned some before this time. But they are still ignorant. You know our practice. If a white man, in travelling through our country, enters one of our cabins, we all treat him as I do you; we dry him if he is wet, we warm him if he is cold, and give him meat and drink, that he may allay his thirst and hunger; and we spread soft furs for him to rest and sleep on; we demand nothing in return. But, if I go into a white man's house at

Albany, and ask for victuals and drink, they say, 'Where is your money?' and if I have none, they say, 'Get out, you Indian dog.' You see they have not yet learned those little good things, that we need no meetings to be instructed in, because our mothers taught them to us when we were children; and therefore it is impossible their meetings should be, as they say, for any such purpose, or have any such effect; they are only to contrive the cheating of Indians in the price of beaver."

—Writings

✌

An Economical Project (April 26, 1784)

To the Authors of the *Journal de Paris*
Messieurs—

You often entertain us with accounts of new discoveries. Permit me to communicate to the public, through your paper, one that has lately been made by myself, and which I conceive may be of great utility.

I was the other evening in a grand company, where the new lamp of Messrs. Quinquet and Lange was introduced, and much admired for its splendour; but a general inquiry was made, whether the oil it consumed was in proportion to the light it afforded, in which case there would be no saving in the use of it. No one present could satisfy us on that point, which all agreed ought to be known, it being a very desirable thing to lessen, if possible, the expense of lighting our apartments, when every other article of family expense was so much augmented.

I was pleased to see this general concern for economy, for I love economy exceedingly.

I went home, and to bed, three or four hours after midnight, with my head full of the subject. An accidental sudden noise waked me about six in the morning, when I was surprised to find my room filled with light, and I imagined at first that a number of those lamps had been brought into it; but rubbing my eyes, I perceived that the light came in at the windows. I got up, and looked out to see what might be the occasion of it, when I saw the sun just rising above the horizon, from whence he poured his rays plentifully into my chamber—my domestic having negligently omitted the preceding evening to close the shutters.

I looked at my watch, which goes very well, and found that it was about six o'clock; and still thinking it something extraordinary that the sun should rise so early, I looked into the almanack, where I found it to be the hour given for his rising on that day. I looked forward too, and found he was to rise still earlier every day till towards the end of June; and that at no time in the year he retarded his rising so long as till eight o'clock. Your readers, who with me have never seen any signs of sunshine before noon, and seldom regarded the astronomical part of the almanack, will be as much astonished as I was when they hear of his rising so early; and especially when I assure them, *that he gives light as soon as he rises.* I am convinced of this: I am certain of my fact. And having repeated this observation the three following mornings, I found always precisely the same result....

This event has given rise, in my mind, to several serious and important reflections. I considered that, if I had not been awakened so early in the morning, I should have slept seven hours longer by the light of the sun, and in exchange have lived six hours the following night by candle-light; and the latter being a much more expensive light than the former, my love for economy induced me to muster up what little arithmetic I was master of, and to make some calculations, which I shall give you, after observing that utility is, in my opinion, the test of value in matters of invention, and that a discovery which can be applied to no use, or is not good for something, is good for nothing.

I took for the basis of my calculation the supposition that there are 100,000 families in Paris, and that these families consume in the night half a pound of *bougies*, or candles, per hour. I think this a moderate allowance, taking one family with another; for though I believe some consume less, I know that many consume a great deal more. Then, estimating seven hours per day as the medium quantity between the time of the sun's rising and ours—he rising during the six following months from six to eight hours before noon, and there being seven hours of course per night in which we burn candles—the account will stand thus:—

In the six months between the 20th of March and the 20th of September, there are nights 183

Multiplication gives for the total number of hours ... 1,281

These 1,281 hours multiplied by 100,000, the number of inhabitants given 128,100,000

One hundred and twenty-eight millions and one hundred thousand hours spent at Paris by candle-light, which at half a pound of wax and tallow per hour, gives the weight of 64,050,000

Sixty-four millions and fifty thousand of pounds, which, estimating the whole at the medium price of thirty sols the pound, makes the sum of ninety-six millions and seventy-five thousand livres tournnis ... 96,075,000

An immense sum that the city of Paris might save every year, by the economy of using sunshine instead of candles!...

For the great benefit of this discovery, thus freely communicated and bestowed by me on the public, I demand neither place, pension, exclu-

sive privilege, nor any other reward whatever. I expect only to have the honour of it. And yet I know there are little envious minds who will, as usual, deny me this, and say that my invention was known to the ancients, and perhaps they may bring passages out of the old books in proof of it. I will not dispute with these people that the ancients knew not the sun would rise at certain hours; they possibly had, as we have, almanacks that predicted it: but it does not follow from hence, that they knew *he gave light as soon as he rose.* This is what I claim as my discovery. If the ancients knew it, it must have been long since forgotten, for it certainly was unknown to the moderns, at least to the Parisians; which to prove, I need but use one plain simple argument. They are as well instructed, judicious, and prudent a people as exist any where in the world, all professing, like myself, to be lovers of economy; and from the many heavy taxes required from them by the necessities of the state, have surely reason to be economical. I say, it is impossible that so sensible a people, under such circumstances, should have lived so long by the smokey, unwholesome, and enormously expensive light of candles, if they had really known that they might have had as much pure light of the sun for nothing. I am, &c.

AN ABONNE

—Writings

෴

A Petition of the Left Hand: To Those Who Have the Superintendency of Education (1785)

I address myself to all the friends of youth, and conjure them to direct their compassionate regards to my unhappy fate, in order to remove the prejudices of which I am the victim. There are twin sisters of us; and the two eyes of man do not more resemble, nor are capable of being upon better terms with each other, than my sister and myself, were it not for the partiality of our parents, who make the most injurious distinctions between us. From my infancy, I have been led to consider my sister as a being of a more elevated rank. I was suffered to grow up without the least instruction, while nothing was spared in her education. She had masters to teach her writing, drawing, music, and other accomplishments; but if by chance I touched a pencil, a pen, or a needle, I was bitterly rebuked; and more than once I have been beaten for being awkward, and wanting a graceful manner. It is true, my sister associated me with her upon some occasions; but she always made a point of taking the lead, calling upon me only from necessity, or to figure by her side.

But conceive not, Sirs, that my complaints are instigated merely by vanity. No; my uneasiness is occasioned by an object much more serious. It is the practice in our family, that the whole business of providing for its subsistence falls upon my sister and myself. If any indisposition should attack my sister,—and I mention it in confidence upon this occasion, that she is subject to the gout, the rheumatism, and cramp, without making mention of other accidents,—what would be the fate of our poor family? Must not the regret of our parents be excessive, at having placed so great a difference between sisters who are so perfectly equal? Alas! we must perish from distress; for it would not be in my power even to scrawl a suppliant petition for relief, having been obliged to employ the hand of another in transcribing the request which I have now the honour to prefer to you.

Condescend, Sirs, to make my parents sensible of the injustice of an exclusive tenderness, and of the necessity of distributing their care and affection among all their children equally. I am, with a profound respect, Sirs, your obedient servant,

THE LEFT HAND

—Writings

࿚

Letter to George Whatley, "But what signifies our Wishing?" (May 23, 1785)

I like better the concluding Sentiment in the old Song, call'd *The Old Man's Wish,* wherein, after wishing for a warm house in a country Town, an easy Horse, some good old authors, ingenious and cheerful Companions, a Pudding on Sundays, with stout Ale, and a bottle of Burgundy, &c, &c, in separate Stanzas, each ending with this burthen,

> May I govern my Passions with an absolute sway,
> Grow wiser and better as my Strength wears away,
> Without Gout or Stone, by a gentle Decay;

he adds,

> With a courage undaunted may I face my last day,
> And, when I am gone, may the better Sort say,
> "In the Morning when Sober, in the Evening when mellow,
> He's gone, and has not left behind him his Fellow;
> For he governed his Passions, &c."

But what signifies our Wishing? Things happen, after all, as they will happen. I have sung that wishing Song a thousand times, when I was young, and now find, at Four-score, that the three Contraries have befallen me, being subject to the Gout and the Stone, and not being yet Master of all my Passions. Like the proud Girl in my Country, who wished and resolv'd not to marry a Parson, nor a Presbyterian, nor an Irishman; and at length found herself married to an Irish Presbyterian Parson.

—Writings

৵

Letter to his sister Jane Mecom, "the bad Spelling ... is generally the best" (July 4, 1786)

You need not be concerned, in writing to me, about your bad Spelling, for, in my Opinion, as our Alphabet now stands, the bad Spelling, or what is called so, is generally the best, as conforming to the Sound of the Letters and of the Words. To give you an instance. A gentleman received a letter in which were these Words—*Not finding Brown at hom, I delivard your meseg to his yf.* The Gentleman finding it bad Spelling, and therefore not very intelligible, called his Lady to help him read it. Between them they picked out the meaning of all but the *yf*, which they could not understand. The lady proposed calling her Chambermaid, *because Betty,* says she, *has the best knack of reading bad Spelling of any one I know.* Betty came, and was surprised, that neither Sir nor Madam could tell what *yf* was. "Why," says she, "*y f* spells *Wife;* what else can it spell?" And indeed, it is a much better, as well as shorter method of spelling *Wife*, than *double-you, i, ef, e,* which in reality spells *doubleyifey*.

"I think," replied she, in her simple way, "Sir and Madam were very deficient in sagacity that they could not find out *yf* as well as Betty, but sometimes the Betties have the brightest understanding."

—Writings

ॐ

From his *Autobiography*, "Human Felicity" (c. 1789)

Human Felicity is produc'd not so much by great Pieces of good Fortune that seldom happen, as by little Advantages that occur every Day. Thus if you teach a poor young Man to shave himself and keep his Razor in order, you may contribute more to the Happiness of his Life than in giving him a 1000 Guineas. The Money may be soon spent, the Regret only remaining of having foolishly consum'd it. But in the other Case he escapes the frequent Vexation of waiting for Barbers, & of their some times, dirty Fingers, offensive Breaths and dull Razors. He shaves when most convenient to him, and enjoys daily the Pleasure of its being done with a good Instrument.

—*The Autobiography,* Part 3

An Account of the Highest Court of Judicature in Pennsylvania, *Viz.* the Court of the Press (September 12, 1789)

Power of this Court.

It may receive and promulgate accusations of all kinds, against all persons and characters among the citizens of the state, and even against all inferior courts; and may judge, sentence, and condemn to infamy, not only private individuals, but public bodies, &c. with or without inquiry or hearing, *at the court's discretion.*

In Whose favour; or for whose emoluments this Court is established.

In favour of about one citizen in five hundred, who, by education, or practice in scribbling, has acquired a tolerable style as to grammar and construction, so as to bear printing; or who is possessed of a press and a few types. This five hundredth part of the citizens have the privilege of accusing and abusing the other four hundred and ninety-nine parts at their pleasure; or they may hire out their pens and press to others, for that purpose.

Practice of this Court.

It is not governed by any of the rules of the common courts of law. The accused is allowed no grand jury to judge of the truth of the accusation before it is publicly made; nor is the name of the accuser made known to him; nor has he an opportunity of confronting the witnesses against him, for they are kept in the dark, as in the Spanish court of inquisition. Nor is there any petty jury of his peers sworn to try the truth of the charges. The proceedings are also sometimes so rapid, that an honest good citizen may find himself suddenly and unexpectedly accused, and in the same morning judged and condemned, and sentence pronounced against him that he is a *rogue* and a *villain*. Yet if an officer of this court receives the slightest check for misconduct in this his office, he claims immediately the rights of a free citizen by the constitution, and demands to know his accuser, to confront the witnesses, and to have a fair trial by a jury of his peers.

The Foundation of Its Authority.

It is said to be founded on an article in the state constitution, which establishes the *liberty of the press*—a liberty which every Pennsylvanian would fight and die for, though few of us, I believe, have distinct ideas of its nature and extent. It seems, indeed, somewhat like the liberty of the press that felons have; by the common law of England before conviction; that is, to be either pressed to death or hanged. If by the liberty of the press, were understood merely the liberty of discussing the propriety of public measures and political opinions, let us have as much of it as you please; but if it means the liberty of affronting, calumniating, and defaming one another, I, for my part, own myself willing to part with my share of it, whenever our legislators shall please so to alter the law; and shall cheerfully consent to exchange my liberty of abusing others, for the privilege of not being abused myself.

By whom this court is commissioned or constituted.

It is not any commission from the supreme executive council, who might previously judge of the abilities, integrity, knowledge, &c. of the persons to be appointed to this great trust of deciding upon the characters and good fame of the citizens: for this court is above that council, and may *accuse, judge,* and *condemn* it at pleasure. Nor is it hereditary, as is the court of *dernier resort* in the peerage of England. But any man who can procure pen, ink, and paper, with a press, a few types, and a huge pair of BLACKING BALLS, may commissionate himself, and his court is immediately established in the plenary possession and exercise of its rights. For if you make the least complaint of the *judge's* conduct, he daubs his blacking balls in your face wherever he meets you, and besides tearing your private character in splinters, marks you out for the odium of the public, as an *enemy to the liberty of the press.*

Of the natural support of this court.

Their support is founded in the depravity of such minds as have not been mended by religion, nor improved by good education.

> There is a lust in man no charm can tame,
> Of loudly publishing his neighbour's shame.

Hence,

> On eagles' wings, immortal, scandals fly,
> While virtuous actions are but born and die.
>
> —*DRYDEN*

Whoever feels pain in hearing a good character of his neighbour, will feel a pleasure in the reverse. And of those who, despairing to rise to distinction by their virtues, are happy if others can be depressed to a level with themselves, there are a number sufficient in every great town to maintain one of these courts by their subscription. A shrewd observer once said, that in walking in the streets of a slippery morning, one might see where the good-natured people lived, by the ashes thrown on the ice before the doors; probably he would have formed a different conjecture of the temper of those whom he might find engaged in such subscriptions.

Of the Checks Proper to Be Established against the Abuses of Power in These Courts.

Hitherto there are none. But since so much has been written and pub-lished on the federal constitution; and the necessity of checks, in all other parts of good government, has been so clearly and learnedly explained, I find myself so far enlightened as to suspect some check may be proper in this part also; but I have been at loss to imagine any that may not be construed an infringement of the sacred *liberty of the press.* At length, however, I think I have found one, that, instead of diminishing general liberty, shall augment it; which is, by restoring to the people a species of liberty of which they have been deprived by our laws, I mean the *liberty of the cudgel.* In the rude state of society prior to the existence of laws, if one man gave another ill language, the affronted person might return it by a box on the ear; and if repeated, by a good drubbing: and this without offending against any law; but now the right of making such returns is denied, and they are punished as breaches of the peace, while the right of abusing seems to remain in full force; the laws made against it being rendered ineffectual by the liberty of the press.

My proposal then is, to leave the liberty of the press untouched to be exercised in its full extent, force, and vigour, but to permit the *liberty of the cudgel* to go with it, *pari passu.* Thus, my fellow-citizens, if an impudent writer attacks your reputation—dearer perhaps to you than your life, and puts his name to the charge, you may go to him as openly and break his head. If he conceals himself behind the printer, and you can nevertheless discover who he is, you may in like manner waylay him in the night, attack him behind, and give him a good drubbing. If your adversary hires better writers than himself, to abuse you more effectually you may hire brawny porters, stronger than yourself, to assist you in giving him a more effectual drubbing. Thus far goes my project, as to *private* resentment and retribution. But if the public should ever happen to be affronted, *as it ought to be* with the conduct of such writers, I would not advise proceeding immediately to these extremities, but that we should in moderation content ourselves with tarring and feathering, and tossing them in a blanket.

If, however, it should be thought that this proposal of mine may disturb the public peace, I would then humbly recommend to our legislators, to take up the consideration of both liberties, that of the *press*, and that of the *cudgel*; and by an explicit law mark their extent and limits: and at the same time that they secure the person of a citizen from *assaults*, they would likewise provide for the security of his *reputation*.

—*Federal Gazette*

Letter to John Alleyne, "Early Marriage" (October 30, 1789)

Dear Jack,

You desire, you say, my impartial thoughts on the subject of an early marriage, by way of answer to the numberless objections that have been made by numerous persons to your own. You may remember, when you consulted me on the occasion, that I thought youth on both sides to be no objection. Indeed, from the marriages that have fallen under my observation, I am rather inclined to think, that early ones stand the best chance of happiness. The temper and habits of the young are not yet become so stiff and uncomplying, as when more advanced in life; they form more easily to each other, and hence many occasions of disgust are removed. And if youth has less of that prudence which is necessary to manage a family, yet the parents and elder friends of young married persons are generally at hand to offer their advice, which amply supplies that defect; and by early marriage, youth is sooner formed to regular and useful life; and possibly some of those accidents or connections, that might have injured the constitution, or reputation, or both, are thereby happily prevented. Particular circumstances of particular persons, may possibly sometimes make it prudent to delay entering into that state; but in general, when nature has rendered our bodies fit for it, the presumption is in nature's-favour, that she has not judged amiss in making us desire it. Late marriages are often attended, too, with this further inconvenience, that there is not the same chance that the parents shall live to see their offspring educated. *"Late children,"* says the Spanish proverb, *"are early orphans."* A melancholy reflection to those whose case it may be! With us in America, marriages are generally in the morning of life; our children are therefore educated and settled in the world by noon; and thus, our business being done, we have an afternoon and evening of cheerful leisure to ourselves, such as our friend at present enjoys. By these early marriages we are blessed with mere children; and from the mode among us, founded by nature, of every mother suckling and nursing her own child, more of them are raised. Thence the swift progress of population among us, unparalleled in Europe. In fine, I am glad you are married and congratulate you most cordially upon it. You are now in the way of becoming a useful citizen: and you have escaped the unnatural state of celibacy for life—the fate of many here, who never intended it, but who having too long postponed the change of their condition, find, at length, that it is too late to think of it, and so live all their lives in a situation that greatly lessens a man's value. An odd volume of a set of books bears not the value of its proportion to the set: what think you of the odd half of a pair of scissors? It can't well cut any thing; it may possibly serve to scrape a trencher.

Pray make my compliments and best wishes acceptable to your bride, I am old and heavy, or I should ere this have presented them in person. I shall make but small use of the old man's privilege, that of giving advice to younger friends. Treat your wife always with respect; it will procure respect to you, not only from her, but from all that observe it. Never use a slighting expression to her, even in jest; for slights in jest, after frequent bandyings, are apt to end in angry earnest. Be studious in your profession, and you will be learned. Be industrious and frugal, and you will be rich. Be sober and temperate, and you will be healthy. Be in general virtuous and you will be happy. At least, you will, by such conduct, stand the best chance for such consequences. I pray God to bless you both; being ever your affectionate friend,

B. FRANKLIN

—Writings

Sidi Mehemet Ibrahim on Algerine Piracy and the Slave Trade (March 23, 1790)

[With this, Franklin's last work, he satirizes his fellow Americans who argued for their right to keep slaves.]

Have these *Erika* considered the consequences of granting their petition? If we cease our cruises against the Christians, how shall we be furnished with the commodities their countries produce, and which are so necessary for us? If we forbear to make slaves of their people, who in this hot climate are to cultivate our lands? Who are to perform the common labors of our city and in our families? We have now above fifty thousand slaves in and near Algiers. This number, if not kept up by fresh supplies, will soon diminish, and be gradually annihilated. If we then cease taking and plundering the infidel ships, and making slaves of the seamen and passengers, our lands will become of no value for want of cultivation; the rents of houses in the city will sink one half; and the revenue of government arising from its share of prizes be totally destroyed! And for what? To gratify the whims of a whimsical sect who would have us not only forbear making more slaves, but even manumit those we have.

But who is to indemnify their masters for the loss? Will the State do it? Is our treasury sufficient? Will the *Erika* do it? Can they do it? And if we set our slaves free, what is to be done with them? Few of them will return to their countries; they know too well the greater hardships they must there be subject to. They will not embrace our holy religion; they will not adopt our manners; our people will not pollute themselves by intermarrying with them. Must we maintain them as beggars in our streets, or suffer our properties to be the prey of their pillage? For men accustomed to slavery will not work for a livelihood when not compelled.

And what is there so pitiable in their present condition? Were they not slaves in their own countries? Are not Spain, Portugal, France, and the Italian States governed by despots who hold their subjects in slavery without exception? Even England treats its sailors as slaves; for they are, whenever the government pleases, seized, and confined in ships of war; condemned not only to work, but to fight, for small wages or a mere subsistence, not better than our slaves are allowed by us. Is their condition then made worse by falling into our hands? No; they have only exchanged one slavery for another, and, I may say, a better; for here they are brought into a land where the sun of Islamism gives forth its light, and shines in full splendor; and thus have an opportunity of making themselves acquainted with the true doctrine, and thereby saving their immortal souls. Sending the slaves home, then, would be sending them out of light into darkness.

I repeat the question, what is to be done with them? I have heard it suggested that they may be planted in the wilderness, where there is plenty of land for them to subsist on, and where they may flourish as a Free State. But they are, I doubt, too little disposed to labor without compulsion, as well as too ignorant to establish a good government; and the wild Arabs would soon molest and destroy or again enslave them. While serving us, we take care to provide them with everything, and they are treated with humanity. The laborers in their own country are, as I am well informed, worse fed, lodged, and clothed. The condition of most of them is therefore already mended, and requires no further improvement. Here their lives are in safety. They are not liable to be impressed for soldiers, and forced to cut one another's Christian throats, as in the wars of their own countries. If some of the religion-mad bigots, who now tease us with their silly petitions, have in a fit of blind zeal freed their slaves, it was not generosity, it was not humanity, that moved them to the action. It was from the conscious burthen of a load of sins, and a hope, from the supposed merits of so good a work, to be excused from damnation.

How grossly are they mistaken to suppose slavery to be disallowed by the *Alcoran*! Are not the two precepts—to quote no more—"Masters, treat your slaves with kindness"; "Slaves, serve your masters with cheerfulness and fidelity," clear proofs to the contrary? Nor can the plundering of Infidels be in that sacred book forbidden; since it is well known from it that God has given the world, and all that it contains, to his faithful Mussulmans, who are to enjoy it of right as fast as they conquer it. Let us then hear no more of this detestable proposition—the manumission of Christian slaves—the adoption of which would, by depreciating our lands and houses, and thereby depriving so many good citizens of their properties, create universal discontent, and provoke insurrections, to the endangering of government, and producing general confusion. I have, therefore, no doubt but this wise Council will prefer the comfort and happiness of a whole nation of True Believers to the whim of a few *Erika*, and dismiss their petition.

—Letter to the Editor of the *Federal Gazette* [unpublished]

References

Jay Carper. *The History Carper.*
http://www.historycarper.com

Documents for the Study of American History. http://www.vlib.us/amdocs/index.html#1725

Paul Leicester Ford. *The Many-Sided Franklin.* New York: The Century Company. 1899.

Benjamin Franklin. A Documentary History. http://www.english.udel.edu/lemay/franklin/1735frame.html

Benjamin Franklin. *The Autobiography of Benjamin Franklin.* Mineola, New York: Dover Publications, Inc. 1996.

Benjamin Franklin. *The Life and Miscellaneous Writings of Benjamin Franklin.* Edinburgh: William and Robert Chambers. 1839.

Benjamin Franklin. *Wit and Wisdom from Poor Richard's Almanack.* Mineola, New York: Dover Publications, Inc. 1999.

Jared Sparks, editor. *The Works of Benjamin Franklin.* Boston: Whittemore, Niles and Hall. 1856.

Edmund S. Morgan. *Benjamin Franklin*. New Haven: Yale University Press. 2002.

Paul M. Zall. *Ben Franklin's Humor*. Lexington: The University Press of Kentucky. 2005.